ADVANCE PRAISE FOR

Southern Hospitality

"In *Southern Hospitality*, David M. Callejo-Pérez moves beyond the confines of existing monochromatic historiography on school desegregation to flesh out the gray hues within both the white and black communities. The central question in Callejo-Pérez's compelling text is the construction of new individual and collective identities during the desegregation process. Even in the face of the entangling web of the Sovereignty Commission, Callejo-Pérez argues that blacks and whites in Holly Springs forged these new identities in a climate of outward civility reminiscent of William Chafe's *Greensboro in Civilities and Civil Rights*. *Southern Hospitality* stands on firm ground while launching a number of provocative shots at existing historiography in the post-Brown South."

Corey Lesseig, History Department, Waycross College, Georgia

"David M. Callejo-Pérez brings the reader face-to-face with the realities of race politics and schooling in the emerging South. *Southern Hospitality* is a lively account of a dynamic period of educational history. This skillfully crafted work will enlighten the general reader, capture the interest of the serious student, and serve as a helpful reference for the historian and policy analyst."

Stephen M. Fain, Curriculum Studies Department,
Florida International University

Southern Hospitality

Studies in the
Postmodern Theory of Education

Joe L. Kincheloe and Shirley R. Steinberg
General Editors

Vol. 153

PETER LANG
New York • Washington, D.C./Baltimore • Bern
Frankfurt am Main • Berlin • Brussels • Vienna • Oxford

David M. Callejo-Pérez

Southern Hospitality

Identity, Schools, and the Civil Rights Movement in Mississippi, 1964–1972

PETER LANG
New York • Washington, D.C./Baltimore • Bern
Frankfurt am Main • Berlin • Brussels • Vienna • Oxford

Library of Congress Cataloging-in-Publication Data

Callejo-Pérez, David M.
Southern hospitality: identity, schools, and the civil rights movement
in Mississippi, 1964–1972 / David M. Callejo-Pérez.
p. cm. — (Counterpoints; vol. 153)
Includes bibliographical references and index.
1. School integration—Mississippi—Holly Springs. 2. Civil rights movements—
Mississippi—Holly Springs. I. Counterpoints (New York, N.Y.); vol. 153.
LC214.23.H65 C35   976.2'88—dc21   00-050658
ISBN 0-8204-5013-8
ISSN 1058-1634

Die Deutsche Bibliothek-CIP-Einheitsaufnahme

Callejo-Pérez, David M.:
Southern hospitality: identity, schools, and the civil rights movement
in Mississippi, 1964–1972 / David M. Callejo-Pérez.
—New York; Washington, D.C./Baltimore; Bern;
Frankfurt am Main; Berlin; Brussels; Vienna; Oxford: Lang.
(Counterpoints; Vol. 153)
ISBN 0-8204-5013-8

Cover design by Lisa Dillon

The paper in this book meets the guidelines for permanence and durability
of the Committee on Production Guidelines for Book Longevity
of the Council of Library Resources.

© 2001 Peter Lang Publishing, Inc., New York

Printed in the United States of America

TABLE OF CONTENTS

ACKNOWLEDGMENTS

This work of labor and love would not have been possible without the support of faculty, friends and family. In the past year, I have traveled through the southern United States in order to write this testimony of the struggle for equality of the African-American community in Holly Springs, Mississippi.

I would first like to thank Darden Astbury Pyron for his timeless effort and dedication to the art of writing and the discipline of History. If it were not for his criticism of my writing and uncanny ability to see the important issues, I would not have completed my work. Secondly, I would like to thank Judith J. Slater. In her, I found the inspiration to express my ideas into words. It was she who introduced me to the wondrous world of philosophy and literature as metaphors for life. In her, I found a beacon for which to reach my potential as a writer, researcher, and teacher. Lastly, Stephen M. Fain, who at times had more confidence in me than I did in myself, for his guidance throughout the last three years as mentor, teacher, friend, colleague and conference roommate. I will always thank you for my career.

Works of this magnitude are not possible without the hospitality, kindness and openness I discovered in the state of Mississippi. I would first like to thank the greatest hosts anywhere in the world, who made *Southern Hospitality* a reality for me, John Morgan King and Amy King for opening your home and hearts to me while in Oxford, Mississippi, and J. Lance Butler, for his endless commentary on the great state of Mississippi. Stephen Budney and Heidi Budney for Schnapps, and the vision that literary intentions come from the passion to love life and be happy. Bernie Murff, the best landlord a researcher and writer deserves. Billy, Spencer, and the guys at Proud Larry's and Murff's, who knew what life was really worth. Scott Lish and Carol Lish, whose dream came true, and offered me a new vision for the importance of living. Russ Henderson, Corey Lesseig and Lisa Lesseig and their beautiful girls for their unwavering support and eternal friendship. Lastly, Luke Massey for living out his dream as a teacher in Holly Springs.

This work would be not possible without the efforts of many persons who I met and worked with, in Holly Springs. First, Mayor Eddie Lee Smith, Jr., whose inspirational career from teacher to civil rights activist to mayor is what this work is really about. Second, Sandra Young and her staff, who allowed me to browse through their vast records. Third, all those persons that opened their homes and hearts and told me their experiences during the integration of the Holly Springs Separate Municipal School District, Al Beck and Ruth Harper Greer, who crossed into the segregated world of Holly High in 1966; teachers Jesse Jackson, Charles Gary, Faunta O'Dell, Donnal Ash, Chesley Thorne Smith, and Herman Young, who did not see color but children; Charles Nunnally, R.C. Blake, and David Caldwell, whom I enjoyed spending hours chatting outside the busiest record shop in North Mississippi; Leon Roundtree and his crew, who were the first to open his house to me and my tape recorder; Principal Joseph Ford, who presided over the integration of the school and twenty years thereafter; Walker Tucker, the current principal who first led me to Ms. Underwood and Ms. Jackson, whose insight jump-started my ethnographic journey through Holly Springs; Greg Gresham, who gave me perspective and encouragement about race relations and Ole Miss football; Bobby Joe Mitchell, whose knowledge of Holly Springs is unsurpassed; Dr. Oliver, who opened Rust College to me; and Lori Swanee, a true southern lady.

This journey work would not have been completed without the warmth and openness of the staffs at Rust College's Library and Archives Department in Holly Springs, Mississippi, Florida International University's Green Library in Miami, Florida, Ole Miss's J.D. Williams Library Newspaper and Government Documents Departments in Oxford, Mississippi, the Ole Miss Law Library in Oxford, Mississippi, the State of Mississippi Department of Archives and History in Jackson, Mississippi, and the kindness and fondness for my work from the *Holly Springs South Reporter* staff, especially reporter Holly Wright, editor Walter Webb, and reporter Barbara Taylor. My greatest thanks go to Gus Palacios, for his transcriptions, and insightful commentary which shed a new light on my undertaking.

Graduate school is where lasting friendships are forged, and I feel I must thank my fellow graduate students for their unending support and motivation. First my colleague, Lilia Dibello, who diligently proofread my work, and Veronica Gesser for her support. Third, my fellow researchers at Florida International University, Tomas Castillo, Pablo Toral, Jerome Egger, Horacio Godoy, Mayra Beers, Roberto Pacheco, Archie and Ziu Lyn, Paul Vicary, and Diego Mendez. Also, Claudia Zamora, Roshann Fletcher, and Aleida Alonso, the world's greatest secretaries. Finally, Professor Robert Farrell, who gave me my first job as an instructor at Florida International University. The work of a historian requires the efforts of an entire staff and an environment of support. I found such a place at the University of Nebraska-Lincoln, where my colleagues made me feel welcomed. There are so many to thank, but Susan Wunder, Sharon Rorie, Betty Jacobs, Clara Hartung, Karl Hostetler, Larry Andrews, and Margaret Macintyre Latta allowed for my flights of fancy with total faith and support toward my endeavor.

I would especially like to thank my friends who were not in graduate school but constantly kept asking me about this work, and wondered what was so important about Holly Springs or Mississippi. It is with them in mind that I wrote this work. I hope I will be able to show them why Mississippi and civil rights were so important for our generation, especially the benefits it brought Cuban immigrants. I dedicate this work to you, Eloy, Pablo, Ralph, Roger and Sharon, Eddie, Robert, Nelson, Gina, Gisela, Frankie, Willie, Rene, Ivo, Joe, Heidi, Laura, and Leah. My History and Philosophy students deserve my acknowledgments for putting up with my endless discussions on civil rights. Also, Teresa, who shared her master's thesis angst with me, and helped me relax; and to Anna, Jenny, Ashley, and Carolyn, fellow Ole Miss alumni and interested critics, and to an especially caring person, Heidi Howze, who encouraged me to finish and lent support to my career aspirations. Also, my neighbors, Tim Mock and Matt Fohlmeister, who encouraged me to continue my work on civil rights in Lincoln, Nebraska.

Finally, I would never have been able to finish my education without the help and support of my family, to whom I dedicate this and all my future endeavors.

CHAPTER ONE

Introduction

As I arrived in Holly Springs in June 1999, the city had just come out of two extraordinary weeks. First, a demonstration occurred over the allegations of police brutality in the death of a young black male. Sheriff Kenny Dickerson's department had been accused of violating Lester Jackson's civil rights. After a Federal Bureau of Investigation (FBI) probe, the grand jury did not find enough evidence to convict the police officers. This action led the National Association for the Advancement of Colored People (NAACP) to consider "economic sanctions" against businesses that had supported Sheriff Dickerson (*South Reporter*, 1999). The mayor, Eddie Lee Smith, Jr., a former civil rights leader and the first black mayor in the county, sided with the police. During the Movement, although the county had avoided serious civil rights violence, this affair led to a serious schism between the black and white communities of Holly Springs that had been building since the 1970s.

Holly Springs is thirty miles southeast of Memphis, considered the commercial center of the Midsouth. Memphis is the largest land shipping center in the United States, and has been growing east at a rapid rate, similar to Atlanta, Houston, Dallas, Miami-Ft. Lauderdale, and other New South cities. Mississippi offers cheap properties and rustic antebellum towns with fabulous homes at low prices, suited for the new sprawling suburbanites who want a taste of the Old South. Holly Springs, however, has not received the attention and money of its neighbor, Oxford. In the 1990s, as Oxford's economy and intellectual community blossomed with the influx of capital and professionals, Holly Springs remained unchanged. Unlike Oxford, Holly Springs has had to deal with all the problems of larger urban settings, such as crime, drugs, and attacks on its schools.

Holly Springs has experienced more violence, segregation, and economic growth in the 1990s than it had in the twenty previous years, including a 70 percent increase in population (U.S. Census, 1990). In the 1980s, the city became a stopping point along Highway 78 for drug traffickers carrying cocaine, crack, and marijuana between Memphis, Tupelo, and Birmingham. In 1986, Sheriff Osborne Bell was on his way home when he heard over the radio that a deputy needed back up with a suspect transporting drugs. As he showed up, the suspect, who had been handcuffed in front instead of in back, pulled out a small gun and shot the sheriff. He later died. Sheriff Bell was the first black sheriff in the history of the county (*South Reporter*, 1986).

In 1989, Eddie Lee Smith, Jr., who participated in local politics since the 1960s, became the city's first black mayor. Smith left Holly Springs in the 1970s to attend the University of Miami. However, like many blacks raised in the South, he came back to his hometown, and was later elected mayor. On the one hand is his past as a civil rights leader, remembered by the older whites and blacks. On the other hand, he is a politician worried about the economic development of a run down city. Smith, like Holly Springs, is trying to deal with the changing economy and politics of a historically divided black and white community that changed forever in the 1960s. He has been able to forge a coalition of local black leaders and white elites who have supported an urban revitalization project for the city. Many of the people who voted for Smith do not realize his past or the county's as one of the oldest and most revered towns for both whites and blacks, for completely different reasons. The Garden Club's spring tour of antebellum homes in April makes the city famous in the eyes of white Mississippi. For blacks, Mississippi Industrial College (MI) and Rust College have represented bastions of education in a place that offered few opportunities for them.

Holly Springs has always been attractive to me. As a first year teacher at Marshall Academy (MA), I experienced one side of Holly Springs. My experiences in 1995 led me to ask questions about my own racial and ethnic identity. As I examined race relations in town, I believed them to be amicable. I could not be closer to the truth, and further from the reality of the town. On the one hand, the relationships were amicable, polite, and even friendly. On the other hand an economically and socially segregated town lies beneath all the politeness. The uniqueness of this North Mississippi town is what inspired me to tell its story. I hope to avoid what Lee D. Baker (1998) calls the attempt to settle past wrongs by writing a revisionist recount of Holly Springs. Civil rights historiography has tended to emphasize the extraordinary and the exciting over the mundane. This work uses social change literature to examine the change and resistance in the Civil Rights Movement in Holly Springs. The main focus of this work is the battle for the desegregation of the public schools.

I hope this work contributes and sheds light on places like Holly Springs, which avoided civil rights violence but remained largely unchanged. The politeness of the formal relations between the races made the Holly Springs experience unique. Although it is unique in terms of the civil rights historiography, which tends to report the sensational, Holly Springs might not be all that unique in terms of what occurred in most small southern towns.

Organization

This section outlines the sources used in the research and how the work was organized. This work draws on interviews of persons involved in the Civil Rights Movement in Holly Springs between 1964 and 1974. Their experiences have been complemented by the use of the local newspaper, the *South Reporter*, and the state's largest publication, the *Jackson Clarion Ledger*. I also use local, state, and federal documents on education, politics, and law, and archives at Holly Springs City Hall, Marshall County Courthouse, Rust College, and the University of Mississippi. Finally, this book depends heavily on the information gathered by the State Sovereignty Commission of Mississippi Records that have recently been opened to the public. The State Sovereignty Commission was established in 1956, shortly after *Brown v. Topeka, Kansas*. It was a state-funded institution that gathered information on all citizens of the state of Mississippi. It served to thwart desegregation in the state. The Commission was a hierarchal web of local and state authorities who used any means necessary, from the law to smearing and violence, in order to stop change in the state. The records for the most part offer general information on persons and their whereabouts between 1956 and 1977. However, some reveal the cooperation of local members of the community to stop desegregation. The key point is that even though the majority of these were white, many blacks cooperated with the state in the effort, mostly as informants. Most of these sources have never been fully examined or used before.

This work is divided into four sections. The first section deals with the historical background of the exploration of social change and identity among blacks and the construction of identity in the South. The second section introduces Holly Springs through an overview of the Civil Rights Movement. This section focuses on the genesis of the Movement in 1960, local attempts to cause change through a boycott of the city, and conflict between the black leadership and outside agents of change after 1965. The third section explores the role of the schools in the community during the 1960s. This section contains three chapters that examine schools before

Freedom of Choice; then through the eyes of black students who attended white schools school during Freedom of Choice; third, as the schools fought desegregation; and finally as they were integrated in February 1970. The last section examines the aftermath of civil rights by exploring two long-term outcomes of the Movement, Head Start and private schools.

This work proposes that the Civil Rights Movement needs to be reexamined. The conventional historiography focuses on the violent revolutionary aspects of the Movement, such as those that occurred in the Mississippi Delta or Birmingham, or Watts, Boston, and Selma. Yet, these were the exceptions. Most places tended to be like Holly Springs, changing slowly. That change might have caused more segregation, but it is where researchers should begin in order to deal with current questions of race relations in rural towns. Second, this work addresses the paradigm of grouping whites as resistors and blacks as activists. In this paradigm, we take the authenticity and individuality away from both communities. Not all whites wanted to stop change, and not all blacks wanted change to occur. Both groups lined up across class lines, social positions, education, and even against the federal government.

Historical Framework

This work is based on six months of fieldwork conducted in Holly Springs, Mississippi. In this section, I will describe the five procedural steps taken during the ethnography study: selecting the site for study, choosing the theoretical framework, gaining access into the community, collecting and gathering archival data and conducting interviews with the subject, and interpreting meanings and writing.

I chose to follow Robert Bellah's (1985) *Habits of the Heart* as my stylistic framework. Bellah's work is a descriptive theoretical project that incorporates the subjects' responses into the authors' narrative to give credence to the philosophical essay. The goal is to strike a delicate balance between narrative and theory. The work will at times be solely theoretical, then historiographical, then narrative. I chose Holly Springs because of its location and place in the story of the Civil Rights Movement in Mississippi. The proximity to Memphis and the Mississippi and Yazoo deltas made it an ideal place to launch the civil rights missions of the 1960s. The relatively small city makes it easy to track participants. The town has excellent records and archives. Holly Springs is also unrepresented in terms of its role in the Civil Rights Movement, unlike the Delta towns.

Antonio Gramsci (1997), Benedict Anderson (1991), and Hannah Arendt (1968, 1970, 1994, 1995, 1998) provide the theoretical framework for the book. Gramsci provides a tool to analyze the political and economic conditions in Holly Springs. The Gramscian analysis will be used to describe the interaction between the state and its citizens; in this case what occurs in Holly Springs at the regional (Mississippi) and local levels (Marshall County). Benedict Anderson's concept of *Imagined Communities* introduces issues of identity. Even though these communities might be imagined, they are very real for each individual who chooses to believe in them. These can exist at many levels. For example, there is the idea of the South, or of the black and white South. These models of community exist both at the regional level and the local level. In contrast to Gramsci and Anderson, the third theorist, Hannah Arendt, allows an understanding of individuals, liberation from the collective. She allows for a bridge, for the individual participant, between the Gramscian social way of life and political superstructure and the individuals in Anderson's imagined community to continue the dialogue during the change in social mores and values that occurred in the Civil Rights Movement.

I was given full access to the town's archives, the Genealogical Bank, the school system's records, the University of Mississippi Archives, Rust College's Archive, and the African-American Archive in Holly Springs. Interviews became difficult as the news of my study spread among some people, who because of Robert Altman's movie *Cookie's Fortune*, are in what Bobby Mitchell, the town's unofficial historian, called "15 minutes of fame craziness." The goal is to first use the school district's records as a way to gain empirical data on the participants in the desegregation year of the high school. A crucial part of the data analysis also comes from the use of the university archives, which provided data collected by the university dealing with civil rights. The town's archives also provided information that allowed me to reconstruct not only the town after 1954, but also the atmosphere in which the subjects lived during the Civil Rights Movement. From these documents, I chose about ten to fifteen subjects to conduct in-depth interviews. The method to be used for these is found in H. Russell Bernard (1995), Dohrenwend and Richardson (1965), Gorden (1975), and Spradley (1979). Since this is an educational ethnography, the work of Phil Francis Carspecken (1996) also guided me. The interviews were unstructured and based on a clear plan. I made no effort to control the informant's responses. My goal was to strike a balance between the oral history of *All God's Dangers,* (Rosengarten, 1974) and the structured oral anthropology of *Habits of the Heart* (Bellah, 1985).

The theoretical framework limited the scope of the study to the subjects' recount of their attempt to integrate the white schools in the city, but the openness of the interviews allows the actual data from the interviews to go beyond the theoretical model I chose. There is the possibility that the schools were not the place where they formed an individual black identity. If that is the case, then I must figure out where it happened, why blacks did fight for equal schooling. What was to be gained? If it was not the schools, what other institution provided black individual identity? However, what if there was no black individual identity formed as a result of the Civil Rights Movement? What if it already existed? Since this is an ethnography of a small group, then the last chapters are vital. How do the subjects' experiences compare to those of other individuals that the literature on civil rights describes? It is crucial that if my question is not accurate that I demonstrate that the experience in Holly Springs is unique to that place, and, thus, warrants further study in another contextual milieu in order to determine its place within the history of the Civil Rights Movement explaining why schools became so important in the fight.

There are terms used throughout this work that need further explanation for the reader. The chapters on schools deal with desegregation, which is the act of mixing students within schools. It should not be confused with integration, the act of accepting and interacting with others (Swift, 1991). The Civil Rights Movement language uses the word integration prior to the U.S. Courts using the word desegregation as the official term for school integration after 1968 (Whitman, 1998; Wolters, 1984).

For the purposes of this work, I defined civil rights as a movement that responded to the treatment of blacks in the South under segregation. It is a southern movement that evolved from black protest, especially after 1948 (Eagles, 1986). Its national genesis came in 1954 with the Brown case (Sitkoff, 1981), a U.S. Supreme Court case that reversed "separate but equal," and the popularity of sit-ins in 1960. Legally, its birth is in 1965 with the Voting Rights Act, passed after the Civil Rights Act (1964) (Namorato, 1979). After the passage of these two laws, the movement reverted to the urban blacks in the North, and the formation of the Black Power Movement of the 1970s (Sitkoff, 1981; Swift 1991; Weisbord, 1973).

The discussion in this work centers on the question of the role of schooling during the integration of African-Americans into the Holly Springs school system and the forging of black identity in the face of the rapid social change caused by the Civil Rights Movement after 1964. This work will demonstrate that schools had influence in the formation of black identity. The schools served to reinforce the position blacks held in society, and only those that were strong enough to fight against the repressive system succeeded in redefining their identity. Along with this question, there are several key issues raised in the study of the Civil Rights Movement and schools, such as the role of schooling in the formation of black identity and the forces of change and resistance in the desegregation of schools. Lastly, two important questions need to be examined for further research. First, how did the attempted desegregation change the sociopsychological position of the black community? Second, how significant was the voice of the black collective in defining its membership after desegregation?

CHAPTER TWO

Change and Place in the South

Introduction

The public school served as the area of conflict where blacks and whites had to deal with the revolutionary changes that occurred after the passage of the Civil Rights Act in 1964 and the shift of civil rights from a local to a national movement. One of the thrusts of the Civil Rights Movement was to force the integration of schools, buses, trains, restaurants, and other social public spaces. After 1964, the federal government began to compel integrated schools. Mississippi became the national battleground of the Civil Rights Movement, as thousands of northerners poured into the South to force the issue. What happened as the schools were integrated? The transformation, described by Hannah Arendt (1995) as "chaos," led to a revolutionary change after the social order of white resistance and segregation collapsed underneath the pressure of federal intervention converging blacks and whites recklessly. Blacks were no longer Negroes. As a community, blacks were forced to build a new identity forged by the pressures of being black in a white society's norm, and not being able to control their destiny (Taulbert, 1989).

Several states' governors were willing to go as far as decertifying schools when there was a move toward desegregation (Woodward, 1974). Decertification was white resistance-based law instituted as a response to Brown that allowed the southern states to label schools unsatisfactory and then close them down, rather than seeing them desegregated (Curry, 1995; Wolters, 1984). Segregation was slow in disappearing because the federal government would not enforce the U.S. Courts' decisions. Desegregation was only occurring in places where racial hierarchies were already fading, usually in the border states (Woodward, 1974). In the United States, racial problems were "regarded as largely a Southern peculiarity" (Woodward 1974, p.64). C. Vann Woodward believed that 1960 was the great awakening of the southern black, as they formed organizations, such as the Student Nonviolent Co-ordinating Committee (SNCC), to help southern blacks take full advantage of the Brown decision (Carson, 1981; Marable, 1983, 1989). Since the act to integrate the public space was ultimately an individual choice, the black individual had to deal with the psychological and social context of being the outsider in the school. Those who succeeded decided to leave, those who did not, returned to the black community. The loneliness of integration forged a new individual who constantly dealt with the resistance of change from within, white and black society, and the pressure to succeed and "get out" from black society, and from white liberal society who had pushed for integration in the South. In the past, black college graduates became the ministers, schoolteachers, doctors, entrepreneurs, and U.S. postal service workers as these vital roles became necessary for survival of the black community (Bullock, 1970, p. 175). The logic among blacks at the turn of the century was summed up by Paul Harvey in *Redeeming the South*, when he stated that "collective racial self-help would come through individual striving, while racial solidarity would enhance the black individual's success" (Harvey, 1997, p. 229). Black individuals had a duty to their community, and were limited in their ability to gain employment outside of the black community, in the South, or in the rest of the country. In the 1960s there was a change in the role that the black individual played in the community. How was the experience of blacks integrating the schools shaped?

This chapter explores two concepts in the formation of black identity in the South. The main focus is on the conflict between the role of black individuals during the Civil Rights Movement over integration. In order to explain this context, this work constructs a theoretical framework using the theories of imagined communities and change. The concept of imagined communities focuses on the idea of place among blacks in the South. Benedict Anderson (1991) introduced the concept most useful in this study. He described imagined community as imagined because although the members of the community might not know each other, "in the minds of each lives the image of their communion" (Anderson, 1991, p. 6). It is a community, because, "regardless of the actual inequality and exploitation that may prevail in each, the nation is always conceived as a deep, horizontal comradeship" (Anderson, 1991, p. 7). Second, the concept of change is explained through the use of Antonio Gramsci (1997). This section describes the change caused by the events that occurred in the South between 1964 and 1972. The concept of place is reconceptualized by blacks as they are confronted with the rapid social change of the South.

Third, Hannah Arendt's (1998) concept of "action" is used to describe the form that black identity took after desegregation was complete in 1974.

At this time it is crucial to discuss the role of the community church in the black community. Although the focus of this work is the public schools during the Civil Rights Movement between 1964 and 1974, the importance of the church as a change agent in the Movement is incalculable. Holly Springs offers a unique opportunity for study because its leadership did not come from the community church or from outside ministers, but from the local school teachers. This is not to say that the church did not play a role in Holly Springs. Asbury Methodist Church offered its chapel for Freedom Schools, and it was the first meeting place of the early Movement in Holly Springs. The church in the city was overshadowed by Rust College, a local black college, which provided its staff and buildings to the Movement. Although the Movement was headquartered at Rust, many of the civil rights workers were members of Asbury Methodist Church, and relied on its minister, Reverend Lindsey, for guidance and advice.

Place

Identity has various sources and meanings. It affects both blacks and whites. For one thing, it relates to the concept of rootedness or place. It also arises in racial conceptions of oneself. In some cases place and race overlap, not only in the U.S. South but in the imagined place of Mother Africa. Barbara J. Fields (1985) takes the meaning of place beyond the physical by stating that it is a psychological condition that "grew up out of concrete historical conditions and interests" (p. 59). For Fields, only blacks can understand what being black means or what it is like to be a slave. This feeling is unique to the American black, and the closer one is to the historical place, such as in the South, the closer one is to the past. This idea evolved from the regionalist notion that southern blacks are southern first, American second, and African third (Genovese, 1974; Jenkins, 1981; Jordan, 1974; Rosengarten, 1974; Wright, 1993). There is a second notion of place that does not fit into Fields's argument. Soren Kierkegaard professed that freedom of consciousness, for example, the lived experiences in the South as a black individual from a black collective, can only be achieved by the individual once she leaves her social context (Beabout, 1996). Thus, leaving the South implies a rejection of being a "Negro," and accepting being African. However, the psychological rejection of the immediate past for a manufactured, romanticized Africa, is a natural extension of the redemptive nature of the southern religion. For instance, telling oneself that it will always be better in the afterlife, and preparing oneself for the afterlife as one lives, is not enough for the suffering individual. This collective action is then replaced by a construction of a past that was taken away, stolen by the oppressor. Black Zionism is a result of white oppression, not against the group, but against the individual, as seen in Marcus Garvey's argument for a return to Africa (Martin, 1976).

If this is true, that the individual is more important in the notion of historical memory and connection, then Charles Peirce serves as the next logical connection to examine the importance of the individual within the collective (Colapietro, 1989). By referring to the great African past and their sudden kidnaping to America, the individual has thereby internalized the oppression of the society as personal oppression. For Charles Peirce the life of one self is inseparable from the lives of any other self. The southern black is not an individually constructed person, but a part, a case study of some socially constructed peoples. The southern black is southern and black, a former slave, whose role is defined by the dominant society, not an African prince sequestrated from Africa. Even that past has disappeared. As Fields (1985) stated, blacks, because of their historical past and their current state, understand what it is like to be a slave, and not an African prince. In America, blacks became slaves, and because of the racial strife that exists are a part of a racial and prejudiced society. Hannah Arendt (1994) explains that group rebellion is not possible because the group has been acculturated in the nature of slavery and oppression, but the individual can escape that mental prison.

The power of identity was not only strong among southern blacks but among white southerners. The Civil War solidified white identity as did the region's unique experiences with rebuilding, and the issue of race. According to C. Vann Woodward, "every self-conscious group of any size fabricates myths about its past: about its origins, its mission, its righteousness, its benevolence, its general superiority" (Woodward, 1993, p. 12). Woodward raised this issue and argued that although southerners believed themselves to be unique, they were not (Woodward, 1993). Real or not, this ideology provoked real effects. Southern identity was based on a masculinity which became the apparatus of a cultural difference as in the case of white resistance. The cultural difference revolved around the idealized conceptual framework of the agrarian society, consisting of chivalry, honor, womanhood and slavery (Gaston, 1970). George Tindall believed that myths like the Lost Cause had a tendency to lay "the ground for belief, for either loyalty and defense on the one hand or hostility and opposition on the other" (Tindall, 1964, p. 2). The Lost Cause was a post-Civil War attempt to operationalize the experiences of southerners after the loss on the battlefield. It was a recreation of their society around the ideology that they believed led them to fight for their land. Robert Penn Warren captured this ideology in *Legacy of the Civil War*, with the term "Great Alibi." "By the Great Alibi the Southerner explains, condones, and transmutes everything. By a single reference to the 'War'. . . laziness becomes the aesthetic sense . . . and resentful misery becomes divine revelation . . . he turns defeat into victory, defects into virtue" (Warren, 1961). The myth was very real in terms of action, as described by William Faulkner (1964) in *Absalom, Absalom!* Faulkner recreates the charge on Gettysburg as if he had been there, experiencing it all over again, hoping that this latest charge would lead to victory. This connection is the strongest bond within the imagined community and the hardest to break. The individual makes a connection to the past through games which are natural outgrowths of the surrounding situations.

John Hope Franklin referred to the unification of nationalism and honor in southerners leading to a new consciousness positing that whenever a "Southerner fought another, he was, in a very real sense, engaged in war. The honor and dignity at stake were no less important to the individual than they would be to an embattled nation" (Franklin, 1968, p. 36; Wyatt-Brown, 1984). The southern ideology of honor caused "[the southerner] to defend with his life the slightest suggestion of irregularity in his honesty and integrity" (p. 35). Furthermore, "however seriously lightly he may have taken other rules of life . . . the Southerner convinced himself that life should be ordered by certain well-defined codes of conduct" (p. 34). Blacks were a part of this fabricated southern culture. They were not immune to its dogmatic catechism of family, fatalism, redemption, social order, honor, community and romanticism. Recalling this notion of southernness, many whites feared that "broader educational opportunity for blacks . . . could profoundly unsettle the patterns of southern life" (McMillen, 1989, p. 90). The social order, black and white, wanted black education to remain largely manual labor-oriented, and unique for the "Negro" race (p. 91).

Place shaped the psychology of black identity prior to the integration of schools. In *Silver Rights* (1995), Constance Curry recognized that Lyndon Johnson's promise that he would uphold the law of the land led blacks to exercise their right to "freedom of choice," in selecting schools under the Civil Rights Act of 1964, although few African-American parents chose to integrate the schools. She concluded that while beneficial to those who "sacrificed" and "struggled" to be acculturated, for others it became a tragic event, as the newly freed individuals departed, leaving behind no leadership for the collective. Although advancement for the group meant advancement for the individual, the opposite was not true. In the latter case, the individual had another choice; to meld into the white mainstream. In the end, the law helped some succeed, while at the same time exploding the solidarity described in the literary works of Zora Neale Hurston in the 1940s and Alice Walker in the 1970s, which helped empower blacks during the Jim Crow years.

There was a mask on the social persona that hid the realities of the society, similar to the metaphor Franz Fanon (1967) used in *Black Skin, White Masks* to describe being black in a colonial state. Fanon described the return to Martinique by a Martiniquais who was born, raised, and educated in France. The man overemphasized his accent and manners, as he believed them to be. The man was treated as an outsider in both societies. In the end, the man decided to act like a Martiniquais in France and like a Frenchman in Trinidad. The shifting identity was not real in any sense, as the man wore a white mask, yet still bore black skin. Curry's and Fanon's examples illustrate the importance of place for individuals, especially when they attempt to navigate between two distinct worlds.

In *Black Boy*, Richard Wright (1998) wrote of his love of place, and of the hate of the people in the same breath. Wright's voice in describing Roxie, Mississippi, or the disappointment of leaving the South to discover the unfriendliness of Chicago in *The Outsider* (1993), when he discovered that the collective "Negro" support of the South allowed him to overcome the hate for the color of his skin, whereas Chicago offered no such communal refuge. Black individuals' identity was based on a definition of place and past in the South, tortured by their membership in the oppressed black caste, as well as their membership in the larger American community.

Identity was connected to place through the references to Africa and the U.S. South by blacks. A southern black dealt with the reality of being from the caste-like South but also looked toward Africa for identity. Individual identity was reinforced by what Henry Allan Bullock (1970) called the verbal protest developed in the early twentieth century and was shaped through literary efforts as American blacks "were to find a new conception of themselves and a deeper spiritual orientation. The new group aspired to reestablish the Negro's racial heritage. . . . The Negro must remake his past in order to make his future. And so they wrote of African Kings, black warriors, black leaders of slave rebellions, Negro jockeys, and the problems of being Negro" (Bullock, 1970, p. 199). The shift in the definition of identity was visible in literary interpretation based on the historical rejection of a past. The change was based on the worldwide movement among blacks to connect to their Zion in Africa. The new identity was a conception of the greatness of the African continent's past by changing blacks' historical place. It was spurred on by the rapid European exploration and exploitation of the African continent begun in the late nineteenth century. In the U.S., Marcus Garvey and W. E. B. Du Bois pushed blacks to discover their past (Marable, 1999). Although they disagreed on whether blacks should return or stay, both men urged blacks to assert their identity as Africans (Martin, 1976). They were attempting to transpose the past as slaves in a foreign land by identifying with Africanness.

The need for economic development in the South forced a change in the region's ideology and social structure. Economic development in the South was an attempt to lure industry, first through the railroads in the 1880s, second through mining in the Alabama area, and third through textiles in the Appalachian mountains (Cooper and Terrill, 1991). James Cobb (1982, 1984) outlines the South's attempt to industrialize, especially in Alabama, and the conflict between the southern mindset, which did not accommodate to the unionism sweeping the country (Reed, Hough, and Fink, 1981). The same was evident in the mill world, where former sharecroppers still existed in the yeoman ideals of the imagined South (Hall, 1987). The rise of farmers' unions and the populist movement in the previous century were signs of the unhappiness with the economic situation.

The race question also loomed larger than ever. W. E. B. Du Bois stated, it provided the central theme in the twentieth century (Du Bois,

1995). The burden of race was the persistent tradition in the economic development of the South (Osofsky, 1967). Also evident were the large numbers of farms, the low production and the low acreage of tillable soil at the turn of the century, as was the depravity that was blamed on the "Negro and the North" (Cooper and Terrill, 1991). Along with the Lost Cause and the myth-creation of the South, especially at is two main universities, Vanderbilt and North Carolina, the economic situation led to a new nationalism based on the Lost Cause myth and the economic depression (O'Brien, 1979), which served to create a landscape that would transform the South after World War II, as well as the Civil Rights Movement (Foster, 1987; Goldfield, 1990; Hacker, 1992; Janiewski, 1985; Morris, 1984).

Change and Black Identity

Blacks' identity shifted as the South began to undergo revolutionary change in the 1960s. The Civil Rights Movement, referred to as the Second Reconstruction, caused a reexamination of what both blacks and whites accepted as social reality (Black, 1976; Marable, 1989). For example, the social mechanism used by blacks to resist segregation in the twentieth century could have served as the structure for change and the social improvement of the black community. However, it was replaced by the individualistic drive for personal empowerment (Arendt, 1998; Ellison, 1994). The key to change was that the entire community had to be helped. The success of the black individual caused the failure of the black communal culture (Baldwin, 1961; Schrag, 1971).

The resistance to change in the South was a long and costly battle between the change agents (federal government) and the defenders (southern politicians and Citizens' Council). Legislation had been passed, court cases had been decided, yet there still was not any change in Mississippi. Kenneth Benne, Robert Chin, and Warren Bennis explained that the most effective change only occurs when the change agent is able to reeducate the society (Benne, Bennis, and Chin in Bennis et al., 1961, p. 20). Therefore, planned change attacks the heart of the society in an attempt to change the belief patterns of the individuals (Benne, Bennis, and Chin in Bennis et al., 1961).

Why was resistance to change in Mississippi so strong? One reason was that the federal government wanted top down change through the fastest means possible (Black, 1976). According to Chris Argyris and Donald Schon (1974), there are difficult and easy interventions. Three issues are involved in deciding which are easy and which are difficult interventions. First, there is the "participants' degree of effectiveness, two, how much power and control each person has and third, the probability of rejection" (Argyris and Schon, 1974, p. 72). The authors go on to discuss difficult and easy cases, the most relevant for Mississippi "was [the agent of change] faced with a client who was unwilling to be passive and doubted that he needs help" and that the agent of change " . . . had many, and/or strong important fears of rejection" (Argyris and Schon, 1974, p. 72).

What were the possible consequences of change in Mississippi? Argyris and Schon (1974) predict four: first, the actors are defensive; two interpersonal and group relationships will become more defensive; three, defensiveness in "individuals . . . and groups' behavior will generate norms that support . . . conformity, antagonism and mistrust" and four, there will be little freedom to search for new and different ways to change (p. 73). As the game became more intense, each player became more protective. Pierre Bourdieu (1990) explored the concept of defense and protection in his work. His model is a soccer field where two teams protect their goals (norms and values); the object to the game is to attack and score, infusing your norms and values on the other side by winning (Bourdieu, 1990, p. 98).

Interaction between southern blacks and whites was unique. In *Black Liberation*, George M. Fredrickson stated that the leaders of the black rebellion were ministers because, unlike teachers or professors, they were not employed by white-dominated institutions (Fredrickson, 1995). The work of Paulo Freire (1970, 1994) and Antonio Gramsci (1997) provide a theoretical framework for the explanation of the milieu formed by the dialectic between the social order and the individual in a time of social and individual revolution. The superstructure of the South dominated its citizens, both white and black, as it dictated their behavior toward each other (Cobb, 1992; Silver, 1966). Liberation was a process that could only occur as the oppressed discovered their social position and posed resistance toward the superstructure, which shifted from the local power structure to the federal government. The most difficult aspect to overcome was the individual's attempt to change a way of life, vis-a-vis the state. Resistance not only came from the social order but from the individual himself. The major factors oppressing the individual were the nature of the political economy and the restriction on the expression of freedom, a built-in control in the southern society (Silver, 1966).

The explanation for the form that the conflict between the individual and the society takes derives from Phillip Chin and Robert Benne's three approaches to effect change, rational, re-educative and power-coercive (Chin and Benne in Bennis, et al., 1969, pp. 38–43). Southern blacks attempted the use of nonviolent means, but that had little effect in Mississippi, where civil rights workers were beaten in the hot Delta. Many began to establish political organizations that tried to register blacks, and northern groups had also united to cause change (SCLC, SNCC, NAACP). The federal government then passed legislation, but that was difficult since "the use of political institutions to effect changes varies from an overestimation by change agents of the capability of political action to effect changes in practice" (Bennis, et al., 1969, p. 41). These change agents assumed that because the law passed, change would take place. Seven years passed after the 1954 ruling outlawing segregation, and no visible change had occurred, as white resistance was at an all-time high (Bartley, 1969).

The power-coercive approach induces change through the decomposition and manipulation of power elites. For example, one major struggle for black integration in the state came as James Meredith attempted to enter the University of Mississippi in 1962. This represented an attack on a symbol of white planter dominance (Cohodas, 1997). Black Mississippi did not take up the mission with Meredith; it was outside forces, the federal government, white-supported liberal groups, and the Courts that pushed for one individual to succeed.

Harry Triandis (1995) stated that "collectivism is a more coherent reality for all of us, whereas individualism is a bit more nebulous and depends on the social environments in which we were raised, our successes and failures in life, and the specific rewards we have gained from individualistic behaviors" (p. 61). The motives of an individual reflect his internal needs, rights, and capacities, including the ability to withstand social pressures. It is likely that individuals are motivated to prove to themselves that they have socially desirable attributes. Performance is an individual characteristic whereas the collective sees performance as a group quality, thus it is possible for the group to succeed if one person has ability and the rest expend effort.

Black identity was never a settled issued before or after the Civil Rights Movement. In the midst of the social change in the South, John Oliver Killens (1965) explored the feelings of black Americans and their quest to reexamine their identity. Killens stated: "Who will uninvent the Negro? For nearly four hundred years the black man's personality has been under attack, his selfhood devastated. Ever since he was brought to this country in chains he has constantly been given the ultimatum: Deny your humanity or perish! Where are the artists and prophets who will undo this white destruction? Who will write all the songs for us to sing of our black heroes?" (Killens, 1965). Edmund Morgan (1998) builds on the concept of the oppressed gaining identity. He suggested that the relationship between the oppressor and the oppressed was a negotiated relationship between human beings. Morgan stated that "it is much easier to view them as tyrants and victims, and to displaced contempt by a condescending feeling of guilt that secretly blames the victim" (Morgan, 1998, p. 16). Victims inspire guilt but seldom respect. Respect comes from actions undertaken by the oppressed. Blacks chose to leave the collective society and integrate into the dominant culture. The vehicle was not of their own making, but the action to choose was of their own accord. When an individual undertakes a task such as leaving his world for the unknown, he is doing so with the understanding that there are dangers that come both from within and from without (Lewin, 1948). Such was the case of those fleeing Europe in World War II after the Nazi threat, without a place to rest that welcomed them. The Civil Rights Movement was difficult, especially the integration of schools, because southern blacks did not act as a rebellious force due to the power of acculturation and resistance from the whites in the South.

When reading this work, the reader must remember that Holly Springs represents only a small part of the Civil Rights Movement in the South, and that many of the decisions made by the local leadership were without the benefit of hindsight. In the end, the Civil Rights Movement in Holly Springs allowed individual blacks with the faith to trust the changing social system the opportunity to discover their individuality and reinterpret their place. On the other hand, unlike the local whites who remained in control of the economic and political arenas of the town, the local black community was caught off-guard by the rapid change, and they were unable to deal with the consequences.

CHAPTER THREE

Holly Springs:
Introduction to a North Mississippi City

Introduction

This chapter examines Holly Springs from 1960 to 1972. I have attempted to paint a picture of Holly Springs that allows access to the geography and economic and political conditions in the town. The chapter begins with a brief historical description of Holly Springs from its founding in 1836 to its height as an important economic center for North Mississippi, and its downfall after the depression and World War II. Then, the physical geography of the city is explained. The city's center, the town square, is different from other cities of similar size, in that the square is crossed by five streets instead of the usual four. This section also serves as a point of reference for the later chapters in sections two and three. Place plays a critical role in the events of the town.

The third section in this chapter surveys the economic development of the town and Marshall County prior to the Civil Rights Movement and immediately after. Although some economic improvement occurred, they had little effect on the social and political order. This point will be evident in chapter six as the post-civil rights political and social orders are discussed. Economically, the demographic shift in the town and the employment of blacks is critical. This part deals with the economic shift from agriculture to manufacturing, and the geographic movement of the black population.

Last, this chapter connects schooling and society. The basis for the economic change that occurred during the Civil Rights Movement is explored in section three. In this brief discussion, I attempt to construct the educational background of the town and the county prior to desegregation, and also suggest the effects desegregation had on the black population and the public schools in 1970.

Holly Springs, 1840–1940

Holly Springs was incorporated in 1836, after the 1836 Treaty of Pontotoc with the Chickasaw Indians who relinquished most of North Mississippi. The first residents of the town migrated to the wilderness of North Mississippi from Virginia, Georgia, and the Carolinas in search of the riches of cotton. By 1836, Holly Springs had grown up around a tavern with an estimated 4,000 residents (State of Mississippi Historical Archives, City of Holly Springs, Holly Springs Tax Records, 1836–1900). Many of the town's first residents came from Virginia and tried to recreate the buildings and houses that were familiar (Smith and Miller, 1998). This gave the architecture of the town a unique style that made Holly Springs' antebellum homes famous (Smith and Miller, 1998). In 1837, the town had twenty dry good stores, two drugstores, three banks, several hotels, and over ten saloons. A courthouse was erected, and town records show that there were forty lawyers practicing in the town. The early homes used the formal porticoes which later gave way to fancy Italian columns and ironworks constructed in the Jones and McElwain Foundry in Holly Springs and were shipped throughout the South. The cotton crisis of 1840 hurt Holly Springs, but before the Civil War, it was the county seat of Marshall County, the largest cotton-producing county in Mississippi.

During his campaign in the West, General Ulysses S. Grant used Holly Springs as his Mississippi headquarters, sparing the town from destruction. However, the town experienced over sixty raids, including some by General Earl Van Dorn, which delayed the Union troops' departure south. The town's buildings also suffered from use as stables, ammunition depots, and barracks. Federal troops, for example, used the fine ironwork on the homes for target practice (Smith and Miller, 1998). Soon after the war, Holly Springs suffered from a massive yellow fever outbreak. The epidemic of 1878 took many lives and the town took in residents from surrounding areas, including Grenada, with the fever. The fever spread to an estimated 1,400 people, of which 300 died. After a population boom at the end of the nineteenth century, the population of Holly Springs has remained static, fluctuating at around 5,000 residents from the last century through the 1990s.

In the U.S. South, the slave system gave way to a sharecropping system. The history of Holly Springs and of Marshall County was intertwined inextricably with cotton. The boll weevil invasion and the worldwide collapse of cotton prices in the 1920s and 1930s undermined the economy and the county and city never recovered. Cotton gins began to close. Light industry, mostly distribution facilities and factories that made parts, replaced them. The Second World War did not bring much prosperity to the town. The rise of Memphis as an industrial center kept most industry away. The growth of Memphis and Birmingham diminished the town's importance too, especially as a railway center of North Mississippi. In fact, the primary mode of transportation of cotton was still the mule-pulled wagon. The majority of the cotton was picked by blacks who were dependent on agriculture, whereas most whites lived and worked in the city.

The Geography of Holly Springs

The city lies about thirty miles southeast of Memphis, thirty miles east of Senatobia, thirty miles north from Oxford, about fifteen miles north of the Lafayette County border, and twenty miles east from DeSoto County. It is the county seat of Marshall County, the largest county in Mississippi and one reason there was a need for a large number of schools in the sparsely populated county school system. Apart from Holly Springs, there is only one other town of any size, Byhalia, and two villages, Chulahona and Potts Camp. The main business of the county was cotton, and sharecropping was the main labor.

The square of Holly Springs differs from other towns of similar size in the area because it is intersected by five streets instead of the usual four. The courthouse rebuilt in 1870 after it was accidentally set on fire by the federal troops during the occupation of the city streets in the center divides the town into four blocks. The major street, Memphis Street (Highway 7), lies west of the courthouse and runs north-south between Rust College and Mississippi Industrial College (MI) as it heads north toward the black area of the old town. Memphis Street intersects Rust Avenue, where Rust College is located. As the street runs south it heads into the oldest part of the city where the antebellum homes are. It crosses several streets where the founders of the city established their residences. If the town was to be divided racially, the section south of the square was inhabited by whites, and the sections west and north of the square were inhabited by blacks. Thus, as will be discussed later, the perceived fear of integration was the crossing over of physical boundaries. Market Street lies to the east of the courthouse and is the other north-south street. It runs from Hillcrest Cemetery, the main cemetery in town, north toward Falconer Avenue, and into Brittenum Funeral Home, one of the few black-owned businesses that still remain in operation.

Van Dorn Avenue, named after Confederate General Earl Van Dorn, is the major east-west street, and runs south of the courthouse. It begins at

Craft Street (Highway 7) on the west, heads east toward the railroad depot, once the center of business in Holly Springs. College Avenue, north of the courthouse, is the other east-west street. It runs west toward the outskirts of town and east toward the railroad tracks. The fifth street, Center Street, crosses the square in the middle, and begins from the new industrial park in the south toward the courthouse, where it picks up again on the north (front) of the courthouse toward Park Avenue, the main residential street for blacks in Holly Springs. Park is an avenue with deep, multiple dips as it continues east toward Holly High School, where black children lived behind the school they could not attend, then heads west toward Boundary Street, at the bottom of a hill. Boundary Street in the west of town is home to many of the city's blacks and is where the water runoff from the city ends as it is deposited in several canals. During the Civil Rights Movement, protest marches either began on Memphis Street, at Rust College, and moved south toward the courthouse, or as most did, beginning in Astbury Church on West College Avenue, and moving east toward the courthouse.

Holly Springs, 1950–1970

During the Civil Rights Movement, the demographics of the town intersected with its geography. In the 1950s, the town and the county were about 70 percent black and 30 percent white. The town had 12,605 potential voters listed in the voter registration records of Marshall County in 1956. Out of these, about 3,600 were whites. The county clerk had 3,214 registered voters, of whom three were listed as "Colored." Politically inactive, the black population was extremely poor as well. Table 3.1 below serves to show the level of poverty in the segregated states of the South, Mississippi, and Marshall County.

Table 3.1 Median Family Income, 1956 (in dollars)

Area	Median (family of 4)
Marshall County	$580.00
Mississippi	$1,198.00
17 Segregated States	$2,122.00
U.S.	$3,073.00

The county's population density was also critical. The total area of the county was 693 square miles with nine whites per square mile as opposed to 23 blacks in 1956. The city of Holly Springs experienced tremendous growth between 1950 and 1960, increasing from 3,276 residents to 5,621 residents. The growth resulted from both the number of whites and blacks moving from the county for factory work. Between 1960 and 1970, the population in Holly Springs only grew by 107 to a total of 5,728. In 1999, the city contains about 7,261 inhabitants. Most of that growth involved blacks migrating to the city in the 1970s and 1980s as a result of the collapse of agriculture in the county.

The demographic change in the county is more striking than in Holly Springs. Marshall County borders Tennessee and Memphis. Many black residents abandoned Marshall for Memphis factories. The increase in both the white male population, from 3,629 in 1950 to 4,462 in 1970, and the white female population, from 3,745 in 1950 to 4,639 in 1970, compensated for the departure of blacks, whose male population decreased from 8,720 in 1950 to 7,153 in 1970, and the black female population, which had the largest decrease, from 9,012 in 1950 to 7,738 in 1970. The county population remained fairly stable, increasing from 25,106 in 1950, to 25,503 in 1960, and decreasing to 24,027 in 1970. The population decrease shows the slow migration of blacks leaving the county for a growing Memphis after the Second World War. The county was also extremely rural, although it became more urbanized by 1970, coinciding with the decline of cotton and the rise of poverty in the city of Holly Springs.

In 1950, the urban population, which according to the U.S. Census only included Holly Springs, was 3,276. By 1970 it rose to 5,728. That increase equals the decrease of the rural population from 21,830 in 1950 to 18,299 in 1970. The figures demonstrate the county's stability. Also, most of the residents of the county lived in the county their entire lives. In Marshall County and Holly Springs, women outnumbered men. For example, for the white population, females outnumbered males by 414. Blacks also outnumbered whites in Holly Springs by 1,090 by 1970.

The employment population of Marshall County also changed between 1950 and 1970. Table 3.2 shows employment for persons over the age of fourteen, the minimum age before a student could leave school in Mississippi. The tables show that males were three times as likely to be employed as females. Also, because of Rust College and Mississippi Industrial College, and the local tradition of the male taking over the family business, there were fewer males than females in school over the age of fourteen.

Table 3.2 Employment, Ages 14 & above, Marshall County, 1960 Census

Status	Male	Female
Population 14 & over	7197	7754
Employed	4904	1865
School	1187	1367

Table 3.3 Employment, Ages 14 & above, Nonwhites, Marshall County, 1960 Census

Status	Male	Female
Population 14 & over	4764	5107
Employed	3066	1033
School	985	1147
Not in School	1698	2917

As Table 3.3 illustrates, the difference was quite remarkable for the white population of the county. Black females outnumbered males by 343, and like the county population in Table 3.2, black males were three times more likely to be employed than females. Black females were, like their white counterparts, more likely to attend school, because with Rust and MI College, they had a place close to home that their parents could afford.

The difference in the economic power of the county can be seen in the tables below, which examine selected professions of the white and nonwhite population. Table 3.4 shows selected occupations for all males in Marshall County, while the second table depicts nonwhite males. Each table lists the top occupations for each group. The areas blocked out correspond to professions that were not yet classified, or that were not top occupations during one census but then became top occupations during another census. For example, manufacturing became important after the 1960 Census with the desegregation of local factories and new investment in Holly Springs.

Tables 3.4 and 3.5 show that blacks suffered from unemployment throughout the county after 1950. The largest employment sector was agriculture, although the number of farms and workers decreased. There are several reasons for that decrease. First, although 80 percent of the population was rural, very few people owned land. The jobs in the cities payed better wages and were easier. Second, there was a sharp decline in farming in the area. In 1970, the county clerk lists 300 operating farms, down from 1,540 in the 1960 Census. The figure for 1970 was 10 percent of the total number of operating farms in the 1950 Census. Third, farming was overtaken by manufacturing as the largest occupation for all males in the county by 1970.

Tables 3.4 and 3.5 show that a high percentage of the farmers in the county were black. That number began to decrease as blacks moved into construction, machine operators, and food preparation and distribution. The two black colleges, Rust College and MI College, contribute to teaching as a significant sector of employment for black males. Another interesting aspect of the employment statistics of the area is the decline in blacks being employed between 1950 and 1960. One reason for this is the transition in Marshall County from farming to manufacturing, and a decline in black-owned enterprises, which exclusively employed blacks. This decline in black-owned businesses will be discussed in chapters five and six. To compare, Table 3.6 below shows the employment by occupations of nonwhite females. Unlike black males, the majority of their work is in service industries, although many listed their work as professional, or as maids.

Table 3.4 Selected Occupations, Males, Marshall County, 1960 Census[1]

Occupation	1950	1960	1970
Males Employed	6330	4763	58.7%
Farmers	3552	1540	
Teachers	N/A	55	268
Farm Labor	1096	1029	
Manufacturing			29%
White Collar			29.7%

Table 3.5 Nonwhite Selected Occupations, Males, Marshall County, 1960 Census[2]

Occupation	1950	1960	1970
Males Employed	4202	2797	3166
Farmers	2745	1186	244
Farm Labor		737	
Teachers			208
Construction			379
Operators			554
Food Work			360

---

[1] 43.9 percent of the workforce in 1970 was below the national poverty level, while 5 percent made over $15,000 a year. The percentages are out of a total of 7,197 males in Marshall County.

[2] Census did not distinguish between farmers and farm labor.

Table 3.6 Nonwhite Selected Occupations, Females, Marshall County, 1960
        Census

Occupation	1950	1960	1970
Females Employed	747	971	1023
Maids	253	335	244
Farm		140	60
Service/Outside Home		127	452
Professional/ Technological		140	296
Teacher			139

The employment data above does not give a complete picture of segregation in the area. Racial segregation patterns in schooling are also very important in establishing a complete picture. Table 3.7 below shows the statistics for schooling for both whites and nonwhites from the 1960 U.S. Census. There are several interesting aspects. For example, Marshall County's average for median school years attended for blacks and whites is equal to the state average. Second, the number of blacks with four years of college is the highest for any county in state, especially one with over 50 percent black population. Third, the number of whites who completed four years of high school is quite high. It is interesting that of all the whites that began high school, only 13 percent dropped out, while only one third of all blacks that began high school finished. It is significant that in regard to the education of Marshall County's blacks, that after the first six years of schooling, the number of blacks who have more education is much less because of the high dropout rate. For example, only 80 blacks completed four years of high school, while there are 2,825 completing one and four years of school. The Census of 1960 also demonstrates the discrimination that kept blacks out of school, such as forcing the children to work and helping their sharecropper parents make ends meet, and the widespread poverty that forced many to leave school. In fact, as late as 1950, the county schools ran on two schedules, one for blacks that closed schools for cotton picking season each fall, and one for whites that kept the schools open.

Even after that was rectified, teachers complained about their students not coming to schools during that picking season.

Table 3.7 School Years of Population, Marshall County, 1960 Census

Grades completed	Nonwhite	Whites
No School	450	62
1– 4 years	2825	303
5–6 years	1885	154
7 years	685	168
8 years	550	384
High School 1–3 years	250	446
High School 4 years	80	384
College 4 years	130	315
Attended school 25 and over	N/A	2573
Median Years in School (Marshall)	5.2	9.8
Median Years in School (Mississippi)	5.1	9.9

Tables 3.8 and 3.9 below help to clarify the difference in educational attainment between the races in Marshall County. The 1960 Census shows that the only four blacks enrolled in kindergarten were attending the segregated Catholic school, St. Mary. Second, of the ninety-four students in private high schools in 1960, ninety were black. This would drastically change after 1968, when the *Anthony, et al. v. Marshall County Board of Education, et al.* (409 F.2d 1286, 1969) case pushed school desegregation. That case will be discussed, and the issue of school desegregation is the subject of chapters nine and ten. Blacks only comprised 20 of the 234 students enrolled in private schools in grades one through eight. Third, because of Rust College and Mississippi Industrial College, blacks accounted for 756 of the 776 students enrolled in college in Holly Springs.

Table 3.8 White School Population, Marshall County, 1960 Census

Grade	County Enrollment	Public	Private
Kindergarten	21	17	4
Elementary (1–8)	5950	5720	230
High School (9–12)	1165	1071	94
College	776	N/A	N/A
Total Population Enrolled, Ages 5–34	7912	6808	328

Table 3.9 Nonwhite Population, School Enrollment, Marshall County, 1960 Census

Grade	County Enrollment	Public	Private
Kindergarten	4	4	0
Elementary (1–8)	4634	4414	20
High School (9–12)	781	691	90
College	756	0	756
Total Population Enrolled, Ages 5–34	6175	5109	866

Table 3.10 below, from the 1960 U.S. Census, also shows that the years in school of Marshall residents in the 1960s was low, even for the state. For example, the white population in the county had an average educational attainment of 9.2 years, as compared to the state average of 9.9 years. For blacks, the average was almost five years less of schooling in the county (5.2 years) as well as the state (5.1 years). That is not seen in the table below because once the two races' years in school is averaged by gender, the average rises because females in the county average one more full year of schooling than males. The average years of education in the county is

the required minimum eight years of schooling rather than a high school diploma.

Table 3.10 Average Years in School by Sex, Marshall County, 1960
          Census

Sex	Total over 25 years	Median Years in School
Male	4905	7.2
Female	5372	8.2

By 1970, a big change occurred. The opening of schools like the University of Mississippi and Memphis State allowed blacks to depart from the confines of both MI College and Rust College. As tables 3.11 and 3.12 show below, there are 233 less students enrolled in college in 1970 than there are in 1960, from 756 to 523. In the 1960 Census 110 blacks studied in private schools out of a total of 328 who attend the private schools. In 1970, over 1,100 students enrolled in private schools of which the majority are white. Second, the majority of the individuals enrolled in kindergarten, public and private, are black, 369 out of 431, while the majority of whites are enrolled in private kindergartens. The nursery program, part of Head Start, is only utilized by blacks, because most whites did not qualify for the program. There are only ten students enrolled in nursery programs in private schools, and those are at CADET, the Catholic private school, which is attended only by blacks. Also of note, the number of blacks in high schools increased, from 691 in 1960 to 1,486 in 1970, as a result of the changes in compulsory attendance rules established in the state, while the numbers for whites remained relatively the same.

Tables 3.11 and 3.12 also demonstrate the changes that occurred in the county as a result of the change in the segregation law, and the emphasis on school attendance. Whereas, whites' median years in school in 1970 were identical to 1960, the county average increased because the number of years in school increased for blacks from five years to seven years. This change is a result of desegregation in 1970. First, in the late 1960s, raising the mandatory age of school attendance to grade eight or 16 years of age benefitted blacks, who tended to leave school early, and money was funneled into black schools to hire more teachers. And second, the intervention by the federal government into the schools after 1968, especially during the early stages of desegregation, through summer programs, teacher workshops, Titles I through VII of the Civil Rights Act of 1964, and the Elementary and Secondary Education Act (ESEA) kept segregation practices in check until the schools were fully desegregated in 1970 because of the danger to the white order of federal lawsuits and the loss of federal money.

Table 3.11 School Population, Marshall County, 1970 Census

Grade	County Enrollment	Public	Private	White	Nonwhite
Nursery	59	49	10	0	59
Kindergarten	437	316	121	68	369
Elementary (1–8)	5430	4684	746	1436	3992
High School (9–12)	1976	1748	228	490	1486
College	591	68	591	68	523
Total Population Enrolled, Ages 3–34	8493	6855	1696	2064	6429

Table 3.12 Average Years in School by Sex, Marshall County, 1970 Census

Sex	High School Graduate	Median Years in School
All Males	25%	8.4
All Females	29.8%	9
Nonwhite Male	11.1	6.3
Nonwhite Female	13.5	7.6

CHAPTER FOUR

Civil Rights: A Community in Transition, 1960–1964

Introduction

The Civil Rights Movement in Marshall County began politely enough in a letter writing campaign intended to address issues of a loyalty oath and membership in the NAACP. After this first flurry, there was little involvement in the Movement among the local blacks until 1963. The only moment of conflict came after an attempt to integrate the local swimming pool, which led to it being filled with dirt. The two most visible black institutions, Mississippi Industrial College (MI) and Rust College, played minor roles in the Movement. MI specifically rejected activism, while Rust became involved to the point of allowing civil rights workers to use their facilities. Rust also provided a safe place for schoolteachers like Eddie Lee Smith who were fired as teachers because of their involvement with the Movement.

In 1963, a local black leadership emerged to threaten local whites with action. Whites felt especially vulnerable over the "Annual Pilgrimage of Antebellum Homes," held in April; they feared a protest or a boycott of the city during the festival. The annual event was a celebration of the white history of the town. The realization that blacks would protest led to an awakening among whites. At this time, Rust College moved to the forefront of the Movement by providing institutional support to the local black leadership. It provided, for example, a place for the civil rights workers to conduct their business. The local awakening was relatively free as national civil rights organizations were not organized enough to dictate to the locals how to conduct themselves. Also, the reliance on local generosity led many national leaders to follow the local leadership. The relative freedom was short-lived. In 1964, with the Civil Rights Act looming, the federal government stepped up its effort in the Civil Rights Movement. The local leadership had created a hierarchy based on the model it had survived under during segregation. That hierarchy collapsed because the federal government favored young, outsider leadership. Also, with the entrance of the federal government into the battle for civil rights, the local whites became more involved as they too had to respond to the federal government. The appearance of the State Sovereignty Commission became more prevalent as a response to the rise in civil rights activity. The federal laws also became more prevalent in the language of the Movement.

The year of 1964 is crucial as it marks the beginning and end of the local and independent Civil Rights Movement in Holly Springs. The local Movement placed all its efforts into a year-long boycott. During the year the local Movement marked its genesis and its end, with much conflict between its members and the national membership and local workers. Finally, the year saw the start of a corporation, Zinj Enterprises, set up by local blacks for blacks. Zinj will be discussed in the next chapter about the year-long boycott. This organization became a bank that lent money to local blacks who joined in the boycott. The bank also gave financial support to businesses that abided by the boycott. Whites were wary of this kind of organization because of their lack of control in its decisions.

Birth of a Movement, 1960–1964

The first sign of a local Civil Rights Movement appeared in 1960 when the Sovereignty Commission reported a letter writing campaign against local businesses in Marshall County. After receiving an order from Sovereignty Commission Director Albert Jones to investigate a complaint from Holly Springs, Mississippi, Tom Scarbrough, Head Investigator for the Sovereignty Commission in North Mississippi, reported on September 15, 1960, "concerning someone writing quite a number of threatening letters to business houses in Holly Springs threatening to boycott their places of business on the 24th of September unless Negroes were permitted to vote and unless all Negro school teachers, whom the Board of Education saw fit not to re-contract with for the year 1960-61, were- re-hired" (Sovereignty Commission 2-20-1-36-2-1-1). The letters had been addressed to Sheriff Sol Cox; Chief Office Deputy Sheriff, Mr. B. L. Moore; Chief of Police, Harold Bryant; the Mayor, Mr. Jim Buchanan; the Superintendent of Education, Mr. H. B. Appleton; and Senator George Yarbrough. The report described how the Holly Springs Chief of Police and Scarbrough picked up fifteen of these letters, "which by no means represented all of the letters written to various people. We could have collected more, but since all the letters which we collected followed the same line, we felt it unnecessary to do so" (Sovereignty Commission 2-20-1-36-2-1-1).

Most of the letters were written to local businesses and asked them to pressure Superintendent of Education H. B. Appleton to rehire the schoolteachers whose contracts were not renewed by the County School

Board. The letters advised white businesses to complain about the treatment of blacks, as they were the ones who voted for Appleton, "as they (the Negroes) were denied the right to vote" (Sovereignty Commission 2-20-1-36-2-1-1). The writers of the letters accused Superintendent Appleton of "being another [Fidel] Castro, and using Castro tactics on teachers whose relatives had attended Civil Rights meetings by not hiring them for another school year" (Sovereignty Commission 2-20-1-36-2-1-1). The use of Castro is interesting. The city had just become a home to four Cuban families who came to Holly Springs after the Cuban Revolution in 1959. Agustin Martin, one of the patriarchs, was a frequent speaker during the decade at the Garden Club, Holly High, Lions Club, Rotary Club, and Rust College, where he spoke of the tactics used by Castro in Cuba in order to come to power. The men taught Spanish and science at Holly High and Rust College (Rust College Catalogues and Yearbooks, 1960-1969).

The letters were printed and some of them were signed in print by "fictitious names (no such persons by the names signed to the letters could be found in Marshall County)." The letters were addressed in long hand in "a disguised manner in order to hide the identity of the writer" (Sovereignty Commission 2-20-1-36-2-1-1). As one letter explained:

> We as Negroes are asking you to please help us. We are asking all merchants or business people. Since we trade with you all. Will you please see that Supt. Appleton rehires all Negro teachers that he has dismissed because relatives attended a civil right meeting.

> We want merchants to put pressure on Supt. Appleton since you all voted for him. No Negro with a college education has been able to qualify and vote. We trade with you. We want you all to see that teachers are rehired and Negroes can vote. If teachers are rehired for next session and we can register and vote, same as white, we are not for boycott. (Sovereignty Commission 2-20-1-36-1-1-1)

Scarbrough asked Superintendent Appleton to furnish a list of all teachers who were not rehired by the school board, "thinking that, perhaps, the writer of the ominous letters was in all probability a former teacher" (Sovereignty Commission 2-20-1-36-2-1-1). Scarbrough believed that out of the few teachers who had not been employed, "a Negro by the name of Joseph H. Ford stood out as the most likely suspect of having written the letter. I obtained a specimen of Ford's handwriting, and in comparing the known specimen of his writing to certain letters appearing on the face of the envelope, there was a striking resemblance" (Sovereignty Commission

2-20-1-36-2-1-1). The report had enclosed personal checks from Joseph Ford, who later became the first principal of the desegregated Holly High, a position he held for twenty years until his retirement in 1990. The investigator concluded that it might be that only one person was involved in writing all the letters to the various people in Holly Springs. The Sheriff's office told Scarbrough that they believed that whoever the "writer of these ominous letters was, he had no support among the Negroes in and around Holly Springs" (Sovereignty Commission 2-20-1-36-2-1-1). The letters threatened a boycott, which did not take place as scheduled on the twenty-fourth of September. Another letter spoke to these issues:

> Negroes died in foreign countries so people can be free. Yet he can't hold a meeting or vote in Holly Springs. Castro tactics. We as Negroes will call a boycott for every store, theater, Sept. 24th, Saturday, for all Negroes in Marshall County backed by a student body of 800.

> If you all fail to help us, we will call for a boycott of every store but Piggly Wiggly. We are not for integration. We wish Holly Springs Police would crack down on integration so our respectable women can walk the street without being molested by white race.

> If teachers are rehired, please notify Homer Byers, Head of School. Where teachers were fired. (Sovereignty Commission 2-20-1-36-1-1-1)

Scarbrough continued to examine Ford, and on September 24 he asked Superintendent Appleton to provide his department with more "specimens of Joseph H. Ford['s] handwriting in order to make further study as to whether or not Ford is the author of writing all of these threatening letters." After receiving the samples, and sending some to the FBI in Memphis, Scarbrough concluded that Ford wrote those letters. Nothing came of the situation, however, and Ford began working in nearby Benton County the next school year. In fact, the leadership of the county believed that the "writer of these letters has no support among the Negroes of that section, to let the matter rest for the present time and wait for further development." On September 6, 1960, Tom Scarbrough, on orders from Director Albert Jones, returned to Holly Springs to inquire about "subversive and NAACP activities in several northeast Mississippi counties" (Sovereignty Commission 2-20-1-14-1-1-1). After contacting the elected officials in the county, including Senator George Yarbrough and State Representative Flick Ash, Scarbrough proceeded to the Sheriff's office where he used

Senator George Yarbrough's list of all known NAACP members of Marshall County. Sheriff Cox stated that he had no knowledge of any NAACP meetings going on in the county (Sovereignty Commission 2-20-1-14-1-1-1). Neither the Chancery Clerk, Roger Wood, nor the Tax Assessor, Annie DeBerry, were able to give Scarbrough any information about meetings.

At this juncture, the State Sovereignty Commission became more visible in the politics of the city. Senator Yarbrough brought the Sovereignty Commission into the county and city because he feared an uprising by blacks. Holly Springs had two important parts, both civil and social, for conducting a campaign to end segregation. First, there were the active members of civil rights organizations, and second, a black college (Rust) that supported the Movement. The Superintendent of Education, H. B. Appleton, stated that "he felt his school teachers were doing a good job and were pleased with their present set up which the State had provided for them and that it was his policy to dispose of any teacher suspected of engaging in any type of agitation for the mixing of the races" (Sovereignty Commission 2-20-1-14-1-1-1). Senator Yarbrough had just bought the local newspaper, the *South Reporter,* and told Scarbrough that the "State Sovereignty Commission could do much good by investigating several subjects in Marshall County." Scarbrough reported that he "felt that one of our investigators should return to Marshall County and check out the subjects whom he would recommend having checked" (Sovereignty Commission 2-20-1-14-1-1-1). Yarbrough was apprehensive about the influence of the two black colleges on the Movement, and he believed that "quite a few [N]egroes whom he considered NAACP members" were presently at the colleges but did not provide any names to add to the list he filed with the State Sovereignty Commission (Sovereignty Commission 2-20-1-14-1-1-1). Scarbrough assured the Senator that he would return to Marshall County during the week, and because of its important location make as many trips as were needed to ensure that there was no trouble in the county.

Scarbrough left copies of state and federal laws that could be used in stopping demonstrations, registrations, or any other "subversive" activities by blacks. After visiting the Circuit Clerk's office, he wrote down the names of the twenty-eight registered black voters in the county, and was told by the county clerk that "no Negroes had made application recently with him for registration to vote." Apparently, most of the twenty-eight had been registered for quite some time. The Clerk also denied that there was any NAACP activities in Marshall County.

Marshall County was extremely quiet after the letter writing campaign in 1960. After some activity during the Civil Rights Movement, some of which was inspired by the sit-ins in Greensboro in 1960, and desegregation in New Kent County, Virginia, local blacks backed away from the Civil Rights Movement. Without much civil disobedience, the county witnessed a few meetings whose attendance was public knowledge and no one made a secret of their affiliation with the NAACP. In 1961, the Commission received a list of the membership in Marshall and Benton Counties that "we know of that belong to the Regional Council of Negro Leadership, which is a branch of the NAACP and are organized to complain to the Civil Rights Commission in Washington– reference Negro voting in Mississippi" (Sovereignty Commission 2-20-1-46-1-1-1). The list included some prominent blacks in both counties, including the President of the Marshall County chapter, S.T. Nero; Henry Reeves, president of the Benton County chapter; J. F. Brittenum, prominent businessman and owner of a funeral home; civil rights leader and cousin of Skip Robinson, Johnnie Walker; and the teacher accused of writing the letters in 1960, Joseph Ford.

On April 25, 1961, Sovereignty Commission Director Albert Jones expressed concern about meetings in the county and ordered that the owners of all cars "parked near building where NAACP meeting was being held" be investigated (Sovereignty Commission 2-20-1-43-1-1-1). The case was assigned to Tom Scarbrough, who was told to do background checks on a number of people and to verify if there would be planned demonstrations in Holly Springs on March 27, 28, and 29, 1961, during the Spring Tour of Antebellum Homes.

The fear of a demonstration prompted a full investigation on demonstrations by blacks on April 26 and 27, 1961. Scarbrough arrived in town on the night of April 25, 1961. He contacted Mayor Buchanan, who told him about rumors that "there were possibilities of a Negro demonstration in Holly Springs on April 27, 28 or 29, which was the beginning of their annual pilgrimage of pre-civil war homes in Holly Springs." The mayor said "he had heard that students from the two Negro colleges located in Holly Springs, most likely would be the demonstrators" (Sovereignty Commission 2-20-1-46-1-1-1). The next day, Mayor Buchanan told Scarbrough that "the Catholic Priest in Holly Springs said to his secretary the day before that there might be a demonstration during the pilgrimage by the Negroes in Holly Springs" (Sovereignty Commission 2-20-1-73-1-1-1). The Mayor "felt that the Priest intended for his secretary to leak the information given to them in confidence" (Sovereignty Commission 2-20-1-73-1-1-1).

There was mistrust of the Catholic school in Holly Springs. The information was received through the priest's secretary at St. Mary's, the all-black Catholic school and church, located across the street from the all-white school, St. Joseph's. The secretary and "his [Mayor Buchanan's] mother were very good friends and that the secretary for the Priest had told his mother what the Priest told her, and both his mother and the secretary thought the Priest intended for the report to be known or else he would not have told his secretary" (Sovereignty Commission 2-20-1-73-1-1-1). Buchanan wanted to avoid any demonstrations or boycotts as long as he was mayor. He had white support but was never as popular as the man that followed him, Sam Coopwood, who dealt more aggressively with the different power relations in Holly Springs. Acting on the information from Mayor Buchanan, Scarbrough met with all the city police officers to discuss steps to take in the event of a demonstration. Scarbrough returned the next day and helped the officers on patrol during the annual pilgrimage of homes. He returned on the 27 and 28 of April but no demonstration occurred.

At this time, Scarbrough witnessed an event that revealed injustice and simultaneously demonstrates the politeness of race relations in Holly Springs. His interest in the case led Scarbrough to record the opinion of the defending attorney of two brothers named Smith who had been accused of breaking a $95 window. Scarbrough interviewed their attorney, a Mr. Farrease, who told Scarbrough that "he felt a Negro could get justice in Marshall County," because "to his knowledge he had defended more Negroes in Marshall County from murder on down, than any living lawyer, and to his knowledge, a Negro is much easier to defend than a white man" (Sovereignty Commission 2-20-1-74-1-1-1). Asked about whether the "Sheriff's department was humane in the treatment of Negroes," Farrease responded that "he had never been extended more courtesy by officials in his life" (Sovereignty Commission 2-20-1-74-1-1-1). He went so far as to say that "he did not consider the bond a good bond the Sheriff approved to release the Smith brothers on. . . . He thought Marshall County officers were as kind and considerate to Negroes and everyone as could be found anywhere" (Sovereignty Commission 2-20-1-74-1-1-1). The case was representative of the white attitude toward blacks. Even without evidence, they were being tried. Scarbrough pointed out in his report that any white tried with that little evidence would be found innocent and dismissed. Instead, the city went along with the proceedings as if the two men had committed murder. Their lives depended on the outcome of the trial.

Holly Springs lacked the violence of Grenada and Hattiesburg (Cobb, 1992; Dittmer, 1995; Bartley, 1995). There were some isolated instances of wrongful searches, traffic tickets, arrests, and some rough conduct with blacks, but Marshall County witnessed no murders. Much of this had to do with the class divisions in the county. Many of the whites lived in the city and belonged to the upper class. There was a small middle class, and a small rural poor population. As far as the black community, it was composed of many middle class, college educated blacks, who worked in mostly service positions, especially teaching. Banks were the mechanism for controlling blacks, as they owned blacks' mortgages.

A second issue of concern to blacks was schooling. Along with economic control, the white leadership also used the schools as a mechanism to control the Civil Rights Movement. Schools funds were increased when there were signs of dissatisfaction, or when there was a call for integration. Section Three will discuss how the movement to desegregate schools was controlled through the funding of segregated schools. According to the Brown II decision (1955), school facilities had to be equal, and schools had to be moving toward desegregation. In order to avoid lawsuits, Holly Springs and Marshall County built the Rosenwald School facility, comprised of three schools for blacks after the original black school had burned in 1955.

Marshall County had five black public schools; Rosenwald School (WT Sims High School and Frazier Grammar school) in the city; Henry High School, Sand Flat, Mary Reed Grammar School, and Delina in the county, two of which taught children from the first grade through the twelfth grade, and the three others from the first grade through the eighth grade. Even though four of the schools were relatively new, costing the State of Mississippi and Marshall County $924,000, texts and other instructional materials were nonexistent, and the classrooms were extremely overcrowded. The student to teacher ratio in the white schools was 19:1; black schools' ratio was 38:1. As chapters seven, eight, nine, and ten will illustrate, white schools received twice the amount of money for classroom materials as did the black schools, including teacher salaries, extracurricular activities, and materials.

Although all public schools in Mississippi were furnished with free textbooks for each child, these first went to the county office, which distributed them to the white schools first. What was left went to the black schools, and most of the time black schools received secondhand books. The Superintendent said that since black schools had more students they had to buy secondhand textbooks in order to stretch the money. Although the schools looked equal in terms of spending per student, that was far from the truth. As with textbooks, equipment went first to the white school at the expense of critical materials for the black schools. Superintendent Appleton stated that to his knowledge "there are no classrooms overcrowded or any of his teachers overloaded with pupils or a shortage of textbooks in any public school in Marshall County" (Sovereignty Commission 2-20-1-74-1-1-1).

Another concern of the Sovereignty Commission lay in the loyalty oath of local teachers. Scarbrough also visited Norman B. McKenzie, Superintendent of the Holly Springs Separate School District, to advise all teachers, both white and black, that they are required to sign the loyalty oath, "as required by law and to make a sworn statement listing the organizations to which they now belong and those which they have belonged to in the past five years" (Sovereignty Commission 2-20-1-61-1-1-1). The Sovereignty Commission was aware that it was teachers who were heading the Civil Rights Movement. In Marshall County, the black leadership came from the ranks of local teachers, including Eddie Smith and Henry Boyd, Jr. Scarbrough also visited the County Superintendent of Education but was not able to see him. Instead, the assistant gave him a list of the names of the teachers, who are under the supervision of Appleton, "to sign the loyalty oath and also make a sworn affidavit listing the organizations to which they belong or have belonged to for the past five years" (Sovereignty Commission 2-20-1-61-1-1-1).

Apart from schools, two other issues concerned the white leadership, blacks registering to vote and freedom schools. Voter registration took precedent over freedom schools. On March 29, 1962, Sovereignty Commission Director Albert Jones sent Scarbrough to Holly Springs to determine if "Negroes were accelerating their efforts more than usual in paying their poll tax and registering to vote." He also visited Hill-Burton Hospital to warn administrators of the "possibility of their institution being checked by Civil Rights Investigators" (Sovereignty Commission 2-20-1-61-1-1-1). The issue of voter registration had always been part of the local Movement. This particular visit was important because more persons were registering to vote. Also, the hospital was being investigated by the federal government because of its segregation practices. On April 6, 1962, Scarbrough contacted C. L. Riggin, Administrator for the North Mississippi Hospital, in Holly Springs to advise him of civil rights investigators with the Justice Department investigating the hospital. Riggin told Scarbrough that he would get in touch with the Sovereignty Commission "if and when any government investigator showed up checking his hospital" (Sovereignty Commission 2-20-1-61-1-1-1).

Scarbrough also visited Sheriff Cox to verify that "no noticeable number of Negroes paid their poll tax or tried to for 1961" (Sovereignty Commission 2-20-1-61-1-1-1). The poll tax was an effective tool in Marshall County, as it was in the South, to keep blacks from voting (Key, 1949; Woodward, 1974). Those who could afford to pay the tax could not afford to risk their position because they relied on the white minority for employment in places such as the schools. The majority of the registrations to vote were from teachers at Rust College. Many of the teachers were not registered at all. Even if they did not depend on whites for employment, home-owners were beholden to banks who held their mortgage and at any time could cancel loans or raise interest rates. Even if the banks would not have gone through with the threat, many blacks were not willing to risk their property. The majority of blacks could not afford to pay the poll tax, and did not dare register and risk their seasonal employment so important to their survival.

By 1963 things were changing. Black voter registration began to rise. In early 1964, Tom Scarbrough witnessed a carload of blacks in the county clerk's office to register to vote (Sovereignty Commission 2-20-1-67-1-1-1). L. A. McLemore had brought the group to the courthouse. McLemore, a student at Rust College, claimed that "he was only furnishing the transportation for the Negroes who were aspiring to register because they did not have an automobile in which to come to the Circuit Clerk's Office" (Sovereignty Commission 2-20-1-67-1-1-1). McLemore illustrates the new activity brewing among blacks in Marshall County. He drove four carloads of blacks to register at the clerk's office. The event was very orderly, and without incident. The sheriff's department and the local police were well aware of the situation but did not act. McLemore was not the only person who brought blacks to register to vote at the clerk's office. The sheriff's office reported that a Mrs. S. T. Nero, an instructor at Rust College, also brought several blacks to the Clerk's Office, as did a Reverend Broomfield.

Rust College helped focus this new activity. According to Scarbrough, the school had been a hotbed for "racial agitators to come in and go out for several years" (Sovereignty Commission 2-20-1-67-1-1-1). The leadership of the college favored integration and supported the Civil Rights Movement by providing houses for civil rights organizations and employment for blacks who lost jobs because of their politics. Rust also hired white faculty, while MI College, the other black college across the street, had no white employees. Indeed MI President Ed Rankin boasted of his school's conservatism; "M. I. students have never given any trouble and when one is involved in any kind of brush with the law, he is immediately expelled from M.I. College." To prove his point, President Rankin wrote Scarbrough, explaining that he told "all students attending [that] M. I. is interested only in giving them the opportunity to gain an education for themselves, thereby better qualifying them for their future places in life" (Sovereignty Commission 2-20-1-67-1-1-1). Whereas MI and its president repudiated any student who did not comply with the school's rules and regulations including segregation laws, Rust paid fines for students accused of breaking segregation laws or being an "agitator." This distressed Scarbrough, who believed that "if the white Methodists of this state, who are supporting this institution, knew these facts they would certainly no longer make contributions for the support of Rust College" (Sovereignty Commission 2-20-1-67-1-1-1).

Like Rust, the local chapter of the NAACP grew in importance in the year. It engaged the Sovereignty Commission's interest, in particular. The local NAACP planned a demonstration in 1963 along with a voter registration drive at Asbury Church, the black Methodist church. The Sovereignty Commission wrote down the auto tag numbers to match them with those taken a year earlier at the first NAACP meeting in Marshall County (Sovereignty Commission 2-20-1-67-1-1-1). One of the cars that interested the Investigator belonged to Robert P. Moses of Marshall County. Robert "Bob" Moses arrived in Holly Springs after registering blacks in McComb, Mississippi. Moses had been badly beaten because of his efforts in the Delta (Carson, 1981). He focused on voter registration more than on integration (Carson, 1981, pp. 46-54). In Holly Springs he visited a local black who was beaten by local police. He demanded to see the patient, who was being treated and "was in custody of the Holly Springs police. It was necessary to call the police in order to get them away from the hospital" (Sovereignty Commission 2-20-1-67-1-1-1). The visit alerted the authorities because it involved the presence of an organized Civil Rights Movement. The visit by Moses set blacks to publicly question segregation and join the NAACP or the more radical SCLC or SNCC.

On the surface, Holly Springs appeared a black powder keg to the white regime. Scarbrough believed that Holly Springs was one of the most "explosive spots in Mississippi for racial trouble due to the fact that Rust College is located there and has as instructors or teachers a number of racial agitators" (Sovereignty Commission 2-20-1-67-1-1-1). The concentration of blacks spelled danger too. Marshall County was about 70 percent black, but more important, unlike its Delta counterparts, which were 80 and 90 percent black, Marshall blacks had a leadership base centered at Rust. At Rust, participants had a place that would provide support, both financial and psychological. Along with the excitement of new legislation in Washington, D.C., blacks in Holly Springs began to be active in registering to vote. The belief among local whites was that the situation would disappear, and that blacks would forget about integration. On March 5, 1964, Director Johnson of the State Sovereignty Commission thanked Senator James O. Eastland for obtaining copies of the petitions signed by Rust students and staff asking the Senator for his support of the Civil Rights Bill (Sovereignty Commission 2-20-1-73-1-1-1). W. V. Blaylock, director of the auxiliary police of Holly Springs, and Sheriff J. M. Flick Ash requested a meeting. On the week of April 17, Scarbrough visited Holly Springs three times to "meet with city and county officials to discuss with them defenses against racial demonstrators and new laws recently enacted by the Legislature which can be applied by officers in making charges against violators" (Sovereignty Commission 2-20-1-74-1-1-1).

The Sovereignty Commission expressed general concerns about civil rights activities. But nothing engaged the white establishment more than the potential of disruptions of the annual Pilgrimage Week. The Pilgrimage itself captures nicely the city's sense of itself, and hence, the white community's sense of racial threat. Apart from being a local white celebration, it also brought economic activity to local white-owned business, such as restaurants and shops on the square. Scarbrough responded because of "rumors . . . going around Holly Springs to the effect that racial agitators would demonstrate in Holly Springs on April 24, which is the beginning of the annual pilgrimage sponsored by the Holly Springs Garden Club" (Sovereignty Commission 2-20-1-73-1-1-1). In 1961 and 1962, similar threats were made in Holly Springs to demonstrate on the Annual Pilgrimage, but nothing came of it. The festival, which is still popular today, incorporated everything that dealt with Holly Springs's aristocratic antebellum past. A royal court presided. A queen, dressed in period clothing, was escorted by a "kin" who wore a Confederate officer's uniform. The entire white community participated. The queen was chosen by a talent contest for Holly High girls, conducted in the gym, and judged by the elite members of the community. Each year, a house was chosen as the central meeting place where the queen and her escort would greet visitors. According to Scarbrough, "rumors were going around to the effect that a sizeable number of outside agitators, plus Rust College students and local Negroes would assemble out at Rust College and attempt to demonstrate while the parade was in progress and also attempt to visit in the antebellum homes which would be open to the public" (Sovereignty Commission 2-20-1-73-1-1-1). Years later, Eddie Lee Smith and David Caldwell recalled the white hysteria at the fact that blacks in town would dare march on such a sacred day. According to both, watching them worry produced more excitement than demonstrating.

Nothing came of the threats for the boycott, but Scarbrough returned to discuss the local police officers' response should a demonstration occur. He advised them to abide "strictly by orders from those who will be in command at all times during a demonstration" (Sovereignty Commission 2-20-1-73-1-1-1). He also pointed out that one person should make all of the arrests of the demonstrators. The reason for that, he told the officials, was "so that an entire sheriff's department and police department will not be tied up in court procedures" (Sovereignty Commission 2-20-1-73-1-1-1). The person making the arrests should also be "a very calm type of person capable of keeping his composure at all times under extreme circumstances" (Sovereignty Commission 2-20-1-73-1-1-1). He stressed to all the officers that "there should not be any eager beavers in the group ready to bloody some agitator's head, but on the contrary force should never be used except when absolutely necessary, as in all probability any police brutality in this state would go against the future efforts our Senators are putting forth at this time to defeat the vicious so-called civil rights bill now hanging in the balance for passage or defeat in our United States Senate"

(Sovereignty Commission 2-20-1-73-1-1-1). The same advice was given to all counties in Mississippi. Much of the experience came from the earlier demonstrations in Alabama.

Since Holly Springs had never experienced a disturbance, Scarbrough advised them that if a group of demonstrators should assemble, "the police first should advise their leaders that they cannot come in a mass group down the streets and highways for the purpose of demonstrating; that they will be permitted only to come in three's and four's, remaining on the sidewalks at all times and not closer than from 75' to 100' apart, and furthermore that they should not be permitted to demonstrate around the courthouse at all" (Sovereignty Commission 2-20-1-73-1-1-1).

Further, Scarbrough told the officials that if "out-of-staters and out of the county people" were "in line" with local citizens, they should be pulled out of the line and should be "arrested and carried to the jail, mugged, finger printed and held on a vagrancy charge until their identification can be determined" (Sovereignty Commission 2-20-1-73-1-1-1). The excuse given to these persons, and anyone else watching the demonstration, was that "such persons could be wanted on criminal charges elsewhere" (Sovereignty Commission 2-20-1-73-1-1-1).

Scarbrough's reference to "outsiders" raises another issue in Holly Springs' history of black activism. With Congress debating the Civil Rights Act came a huge upsurge in public and media interest in the South's racial mores, and with that a huge influx of "outside agitators." In 1961 Freedom Riders, for example, had instigated a new form of attack on Massive Resistance. For the first time waves of non-Southerners entered the Civil Rights Movement. The media followed them. Pictures of demonstrators being attacked were broadcast to the entire nation, and provoked outrage everywhere (Marable, 1984, pp. 72-73, 81). Aware of the publicity, Scarbrough urged caution. He pointed out that in the course of demonstrations, "which probably will occur in Marshall County this year, mixed groups will be riding around in the city and county together" (Sovereignty Commission 2-20-1-73-1-1-1). He specified that was not a violation of the law, but if the "officers could stop such groups to determine if they had a title to the automobile in which they were riding and if their other credentials were in order," it would slow the process (Sovereignty Commission 2-20-1-73-1-1-1). Scarbrough also anticipated the events that would take place. He told the officials that the most common event would be "mixed groups trying to integrate white restaurants, motels, etc"

(Sovereignty Commission 2-20-1-73-1-1-1). He advised city and county officials to tell the proprietors of such places to request the intruders to leave their places of business as they do not serve mixed groups or colored, and further if the said groups do not leave that the proprietor should call the sheriff's department or police department and upon the arrival of the official at the place of business which is being trespassed upon, the proprietor should tell the official in the presence of the agitators that his place of business is not a place for integrated groups or Negroes to be served and request them to leave again (Sovereignty Commission 2-20-1-73-1-1-1).

If this did not cause them to leave, Scarbrough told the officials that the officer should arrest them and charge them with "trespassing and with whatever offense they may have committed" (Sovereignty Commission 2-20-1-73-1-1-1). Scarbrough also discussed a boycott and what to do in order to resolve the matter. Of all the possible methods of disobedience, the boycott was the most feared, since 70 percent of Marshall was black and they provided the bulk of the business on the square.

The Commission was very astute in handling the Civil Rights Movement. The problem, as Scarbrough observed, was that the local authorities usually let emotions get in the way of the law. He emphasized that the state had recently passed laws which could be used effectively against racial demonstrators and others that had been passed by previous Legislatures concerning integration. Scarbrough gave officials a list of the laws and when and where they were appropriate. The Massive Resistance of Mississippi was more organized than the civil rights organizations, but the state had very little control over local officials. The main reason that integration in Holly Springs took so long and went relatively unnoticed was that the white leadership understood the law and used it to its advantage. The leaders rejected violence and force. In Hattiesburg and in Jackson, elementary students were chased and attacked by rowdy white teenagers as white women stood by and cheered (Cobb, 1992; Wolters, 1984). That situation would have been unthinkable in Holly Springs. The well-natured white community of Holly Springs abided by the unwritten rules of Massive Resistance, as well as could have been hoped by the Sovereignty Commission. They used the law before force. They used their social, economic, and political power over the black community, rarely resorting to violence. The Sheriff's Office took "demonstrators" for talks into the county but never murdered anyone involved in the Movement. The white community did not counteract the demonstrators with violence, choosing instead to sue and pressure individual blacks with more coercive methods, such as threatening to take away their work.

Despite their preparations, no demonstrations occurred and the 1964 Pilgrimage took place without incident. Still local officials worried about the events at Rust, namely the funding of the North Mississippi headquarters of the Civil Rights Organization Council of Federated Organizations (COFO) across the street on Rust College property at 200 Rust Avenue. On June 1 and 2, 1964, Scarbrough returned to Marshall County to query Rust President E. A. Smith concerning the college's role in the demonstrations during the summer of 1964. Smith managed to avoid the interview. His secretary stated that "Smith had gone to Memphis, Tennessee, on business" (Sovereignty Commission 2-20-1-76-1-1-1). Smith never perjured himself, he just could not be found, and thus never had to answer questions about his school's involvement in the Civil Rights Movement. Scarbrough talked to only one administrator, Dean Waters, who also sidestepped the issue because "he felt that responsibility was entirely President Smith's," Scarbrough reported (Sovereignty Commission 2-20-1-76-1-1-1).

The Commission investigator continued to scrutinize the college. The presence of fifteen to twenty white students staying at Rust distressed him. "These students, I am sure, will be expected to instruct in the freedom schools which are to be a part of the Mississippi Project this summer" (Sovereignty Commission 2-20-1-76-1-1-1). Most of the students had come from Miami University in Ohio to participate in the Mississippi Project, which was an attempt to register blacks to vote. In Holly Springs the Project was headed by SNCC field agents Frank Smith and Robert Moses. Many of the white college students were brought in to be instructors for local blacks taking the literacy test that was needed in the voter registration drive. The local leadership tolerated these whites because of the influence and respect SNCC field secretary Frank Smith, who was from Holly Springs, had in the black and white communities. Because of tradition and Robert Moses, the NAACP was the most influential national civil rights organization in the town, and all the leadership belonged to it. In Holly Springs, civil rights organizations were not influential unless they fit into the town's Civil Rights Movement hierarchy, which placed local movement before national ones. Holly Springs served as starting point for the Movement in the Delta. Civil rights workers began arriving from Memphis in 1964. Holly Springs and Rust were safe to train the white workers before sending them into the violent Delta counties.

Mississippi Freedom Summer, in 1964, marked a significant turning point in the civil rights campaign in Holly Springs. The "fifteen to twenty" white students from Ohio staying at Rust College were the catalyst in the Movement. The white staff arrived to work at the Freedom Schools that Frank Smith was setting up in the county (Dittmer, 1995). Perhaps more critically, the presence of the "outsiders" galvanized the white community to action, generally against Rust College, more specifically against its president. This campaign took two directions. First was to discredit the outsiders, Rust College, and President Smith, by associating them with racial, sexual, and social deviancy.

Second, in order to discredit Rust, the college and the civil rights campaign was associated with Communism. Holly Springs was a typical Southern town, lining up behind the war effort against Communism in Southeast Asia. The literature of both blacks and whites refers to the tactics used by the other group as "Castro-like" or "Iron Curtain." This worked with special power among the whites. On July 23, 1964, Investigator Scarbrough reportedly visited Senator George Yarbrough of Red Banks, owner of the *South Reporter* who planned a feature story on "known communists who are affiliated with the Mississippi Project and who have been active in Marshall County" (Sovereignty Commission 2-20-2-2-1-1-1). Scarbrough assisted Yarbrough's campaign. He carried reports which he had "personally made which I felt would aid the editor in his item concerning communist activities in Mississippi and in Marshall County" (Sovereignty Commission 2-20-2-2-1-1-1). In addition to his own personal investigations, he reported, "I gave him other documented articles concerning known communists, who have been active in what is known as the 'Mississippi Project'" (Sovereignty Commission 2-20-2-2-1-1-1).

Rust College teachers and students had furnished a large share of the leadership in the successful boycott in Benton County. The Commission estimated that the boycott by the "Negro school has been 90 percent effective" (Sovereignty Commission 2-20-2-37-1-1-1). In 1965, COFO was also operating five freedom schools in the neighboring Benton County, an extremely rural area. The investigator reported that the Freedom Schools "teach very little out of the regular prescribed text books but spend most of their time teaching Negro history and hate against the white race and rebellion against any authority" (Sovereignty Commission 2-20-2-37-1-1-

1). Local whites, however, seemed less worried than the Sovereignty Commission. The local whites believed that the blacks would not take any drastic action. The perceptions of the locals seemed to be in line with the process of being polite. No one raised it as an issue. It was not any different than all the other black businesses in town.

The Freedom School in Marshall County met at Holly Springs, in Asbury Chapel, where their slogan was "One Man–one vote!" (Sovereignty Commission 2-20-2-5-1-1-1). Their pamphlets advertised that in order to be a first class citizen, the person must first register to vote. Classes were held at 8 A.M. on how to register and circumvent the newly placed resistance obstacles, such as reading tests. After class, selected citizens would march to the courthouse on the square, about one mile away, and attempt to register. The time and day were significant to the commercial traffic of Holly Springs. On Friday afternoons the square was filled with whites, mainly women and their children who were shopping, as opposed to Saturday, which belonged to the black residents. On Friday afternoon city offices were understaffed and not busy. The activists wanted blacks to register with the newly formed Mississippi Freedom Democratic Party. Prior to the boycott, Robinson sent out letters on behalf of the United League of Marshall County (UL) stating that "We have check [sic] the registration books but we was unable to fine your name. If you have registered, or if you have not, please go by the court house and check the book for your name. Please cooperate with us; we are trying to get all of our people registered to vote" (Rust College Archives). The signed letter was followed by a second notice for a petition signed by Robinson and Henry Boyd stating the power of controlling 70 percent of the vote in Marshall County. The letter read:

> In the last election you asked for and received our help, without, which you could not have been elected. We now seek your help in the interest of the National Democratic Party–the Humphrey-Muskie ticket. We will not support any man who runs for office in the future who votes against us in the election, because we feel that you owe it to yourselves and to Marshall County to maintain the good relations we now have between the races, and this can only be maintained if the Democratic are re-elected.
>
> This is not a threat; this is a request for sound judgement and considered deliberation of your opinion in the matter. We are not against the white people, please do not be against us because we happen to be Negro people. Our country has done well under the Democratic party–let's not destroy our well-being with hate.

We have provided a place for you to sign this letter as an endorser of the Humphrey-Muskie ticket. If we do not receive the letter signed by return mail, we will know you are against us. (Rust College Archives)

The movement, led by the established front of the United League of Marshall County (UL), was said to ostracize anyone who expressed opposition to their type of operation. Scarbrough reported that blacks were intimidated which he could never corroborate with any evidence. This second phase of the Movement, immediately after the passage of the Civil Rights Act in 1964, represented a shift in philosophy. This phase was more militant and asked blacks to take sides. Along with the ideological shift, came the influence of national civil rights organizations and the federal government. The UL, the younger segment of the Movement, was also not afraid to rattle local traditions.

The shift in the Movement also invited in northern lawyers who understood the new federal legislation. These outsiders were not afraid of challenging the local law and power elite. Scarbrough assumed that "this group was to be spearheaded and led by Larry Rubin, from Philadelphia, Pennsylvania, who has been exposed in previous run-ins being a young communist." Rubin's career in Holly Springs consisted of defending arrested civil rights workers from what he labeled "drummed up charges." The local white leadership believed Rubin to be the "main ramrod behind the voter registration drive in Holly Springs" (Sovereignty Commission 2-20-2-2-1-1-1). Sheriff Flick Ash went to Asbury and advised "Rubin and his group of Negro cohorts that a mass march to the courthouse would not be permitted." Ash also instructed Rubin and "his group that if they insisted on coming in large numbers they would be arrested. . . . So long as they came in an orderly, quiet manner they could proceed to take the voter registration test just like everybody else" (Sovereignty Commission 2-20-2-2-1-1-1). He advised the leaders that the test "was available to all of those who were interested in taking it everyday at the courthouse and it was not necessary to put on a big show." Sheriff Ash actually persuaded the "agitators" to comply with the "request in not coming to the courthouse in groups of more than four" (Sovereignty Commission 2-20-2-2-1-1-1).

Although no incidents took place, around twenty-five or thirty blacks came to the courthouse to take the voter registration test in the spring of 1964 (Sovereignty Commission 2-20-2-2-1-1-1). The voter registration drive began a week earlier with a poster announcing the registration drive, put out by COFO, which did not plan to continue the voter registration drive the following Saturday or Monday. COFO also put out a circular announcing a meeting at the Parker Schoolhouse, south of Byhalia, on Monday, July 27 (Sovereignty Commission 2-20-2-5-1-1-1), but COFO had to change the plans for this meeting after Superintendent of Education of Marshall County H. B. Appleton "forbade the meeting to be held in the school house" (Sovereignty Commission 2-20-2-2-1-1-1). In the meeting, delegates for the Freedom Democratic Party were elected to represent Marshall County in the state meeting, which was to be held in Jackson to elect delegates to send to the National Democratic Convention in Atlantic City.

Several aspects of Scarbrough's reports are interesting. He is not as concerned with the events in Holly Springs as the locals. He does a good job in calming local hysteria. The local hysteria about integration is referred to by Ruth Greer in an interview thirty years later. She reports that she felt much of the hatred came from these local people who believed that blacks were stepping out of their place and taking something that they were not entitled to take. Scarbrough was very cautious, and understood that attention called to his area would lead to more work. In the town of Greenwood, the local investigator did not interfere with the local politics; allowing the locals to take the brutal retaliation toward blacks. The politeness of Holly Springs is evident in the lack of interference from the local police when blacks attempted to register. In multiple interviews of blacks conducted in 1999, it was revealed that they felt safe when they registered to vote, or when they voted in elections. This was not the case in other parts of the state where brutal attacks occurred when blacks attempted to register (Bartley, 1995; Carson, 1981; Marable, 1984).

Despite resistance of the local whites, Larry Rubin succeeded in bringing black voter registrants to the courthouse. Rubin's address book was stolen, and according to Scarbrough, "Senator Jim Eastland exposed [it] as being filled with names and addresses of known communists" (Sovereignty Commission 2-20-2-2-1-1-1). Rubin filed a complaint with the Justice Department about his civil rights being violated by Sheriff Ash, his deputies, and Scarbrough. This led to an FBI probe into the sheriff's department and Scarbrough. Angered by Rubin's accusations and his inability to arrest him, Scarbrough decided to keep around the clock surveillance on the attorney (Sovereignty Commission 2-20-2-2-1-1-1). Although he was harassed, Rubin did not experience the attacks other civil rights lawyers experienced in other parts of Mississippi. The Commission followed up the campaign of negative campaigning against Rust by spreading rumors on cohabitation of the races, race baiting and sexual delinquency of blacks. Rumors spread around Holly Springs by the Commission centered around the "indecent conduct by Negro males and white females, who are traveling about over this state" (Sovereignty Commission 2-20-2-2-1-1-1). A statement reported to Scarbrough said "it is obvious that the white male and female outside invaders are carrying this conduct on to infuriate our citizens," and led the investigator to advise all county and city officials to "keep cool heads during this summer's crisis and to prevent, so far as is humanly possible, acts of violence which can be avoided of course, they are advised to do this in a legal way without sacrificing any of our customs and traditions" (Sovereignty Commission 2-20-2-2-1-1-1). No acts of violence occurred as few whites ventured into Rust College. Thus, it appears that the rumors were sometimes exaggerated without any corroborating evidence. For local whites, the cohabitation of blacks and whites in the same house was appalling. Scarbrough tried to expose one such person, Elwood Berry, a white graduate student at the University of Ohio from Dayton, Ohio, who was staying in COFO headquarters at 100 Rust Street, and "said to be Larry Rubin's bodyguard" (Sovereignty Commission 2-20-2-2-1-1-1).

Scarbrough assisted local white resistence in various ways. He gave the Sheriff's office copies of new state laws passed "concerning racial agitation, riots, boycotts, etc." The "laws have been compiled by this department along with other laws relating to the same subjects which had been passed by previous legislatures" (Sovereignty Commission 2-20-2-2-1-1-1). Scarbrough also praised and encouraged locals. "Everywhere I have been," he relates, "local officers are doing a magnificent job in combating these Mississippi project communist and beatnik outside invaders" (Sovereignty Commission 2-20-2-2-1-1-1).

With Mississippi Summer and its influx of northern white students, the appearance of outside authorities like Larry Rubin, and most of all, increasing federal attention to local issues, the Civil Rights Movement took a radically different form. If perhaps necessary for success of the black political rights, these forces undermined the authority of local blacks in Marshall County. The fear of integration and black votes began to set into the white community of Holly Springs. It was these outside forces that had hastened the end of segregation in Holly Springs but also took the mantle of leadership from local blacks. Attorneys and students from the North who came with the support of the federal government and with an understanding of new federal laws advised the black leadership on actions to take. The relative autonomy that local leaders had enjoyed gave way to a group of outside forces that understood the new legislation. This went beyond local control. Also, whites faced similar difficulty in securing local control as they had to rely on the state sources to combat the new federal legislation. In 1964, civil rights was no longer a local issue, or a state issue or even a southern issue. It was now a national concern. The sudden federal push left blacks with little control as the federal government became an active participant in change, thereby leaving a void between the old conservative leadership and the new emerging post-Brown leadership. The new leadership was not cognizant of the pre-Brown days. Nor was it as cautious about stepping on the toes of the white establishment (Dittmer, 1995; Marable, 1984). The ensuing years after Freedom Summer of 1964 left the black leadership in constant turmoil as the aging leadership of the 1950s gradual-change approach was questioned by the young leadership, who, spurred on by the lawyers and the federal government, demanded immediate change. Whites were also faced with the decision to continue Massive Resistance in the face of the new, younger black leadership, outsiders familiar with federal legislation, and the involvement of the U.S. Courts in integration.

CHAPTER FIVE

Boycott: Expression of Power, 1965–1974

Well see, those boycotts arose from all . . . we boycotted all the
stores . . . see we boycotted the stores for one solid year. . . .
—David Caldwell (June 28, 1999)

Introduction

If voter registration was the focus of the black movement in 1964, events took a different turn the next year when the black community inaugurated a year-long economic boycott of white business in Holly Springs. Since 1961, the fear and threat of boycotts had permeated Holly Springs's white and black communities. They never occurred. Black leaders Eddie Smith and Skip Robinson believed they lacked support to sustain a mass movement of passive resistance. During the last months of 1964, however, the Marshall County Citizens for Progress recruited members who could be relied on to participate in a boycott. They established Zinj Enterprises to sustain their endeavor financially. They also kept whites at arm's length, including northern black and white students residing at Rust College.

Zinj Enterprises

Late in 1964, Tom Scarbrough began an investigation of Zinj Enterprises, Inc., a company operating from Rust College. Local blacks had established Zinj to provide black businesses with an economic and political organization that sustained their interests. Zinj was purely local. It was a local response to the change from outside civil rights organizations, federal legislation, and the upswing of white Massive Resistance. Under the Articles of Incorporation, Zinj's specific purpose was to "own, operate and manage a line of business consisting of general merchandise stores including items of appliances, dry goods, groceries, service stations and any other necessary businesses incidental to the servicing of our customers" (Sovereignty Commission 2-20-2-34-2-1-1).

The Articles of Incorporation originally read "Community Enterprises, Incorporated"; however, the word "Community" had been struck out and "Zinj" written in instead. The word "community" would lead to an association with the group founded by civil rights leaders Eddie Lee Smith,

Henry Boyd, Jr., and Skip Robinson. This group led a year-long boycott of white businesses in 1965. Upset with the secretive nature of Zinj, Scarbrough concluded that "from what they have filed, one must conclude they intend to operate any kind of business which they feel will be profitable to the corporation" (Sovereignty Commission 2-20-2-34-2-1-1).

The first plans for a boycott appear, paradoxically, in the records of the Sovereignty Commission, that opposed, of course, everything about the search for black rights. On November 3, 1964, Scarbrough investigated the ownership of Zinj Enterprises, which had received a charter from the secretary of state of the state of Mississippi to "form a corporation under date of 17th day of February, 1964, and which allegedly is composed of all Negro interested parties" (Sovereignty Commission 2-20-2-34-2-1-1). The investigator believed that Zinj intended to "cater to all Negro business and to encourage Negro business to cater to them by boycotting the white merchants of Holly Springs, Mississippi" (Sovereignty Commission 2-20-2-34-2-1-1). The corporation was attempting to revitalize black business in the area by becoming a lending institution and supporting a mechanism for blacks during the boycott.

In order to comply with state laws, anyone who was interested in obtaining a charter to do business in the state of Mississippi, and in any specific county, "must run an advertisement in the county newspaper in the county which the corporation is to be located for three issues" (Sovereignty Commission 2-20-2-34-2-1-1). Elouise Wolfe, who ran advertisements for the paper, stated that "no such advertisement of intention had been run by the Zinj Enterprise Corporation" (Sovereignty Commission 2-20-2-34-2-1-1). Minnie Mae McAlexander, the Chancery Clerk of Marshall County, was asked "to determine whether or not a copy of the charter granted by the state had been enrolled in the record books according to law, and whether or not a copy of the intentions of the corporation to sell stock in the corporation, both common and preferred had been filed in the clerk's office" (Sovereignty Commission 2-20-2-34-2-1-1). The charter had been registered with the chancery clerk, and the "intentions of the corporation to sell stock in the stock company was also registered in the clerk's office" (Sovereignty Commission 2-20-2-34-2-1-1). The information was recorded on February 21, 1964, and all officers listed as president, vice president, secretary, treasurer, and directors were Rust College faculty. Paradoxically, much of what remains of Zinj Enterprises, or what we know, comes from the Sovereignty Commission which, of course, opposed the entire enterprise of what it stood for.

After checking with McAlexander, Scarbrough visited Sheriff Ash concerning "this proposed new corporation in Holly Springs and none of them had heard anything about it" (Sovereignty Commission 2-20-2-34-2-1-1). Ash suggested to Scarbrough that "for the time being, not to contact any of the officers in Zinj Enterprises as they preferred that they would sell some stock since they had not complied with the law and, thus, they would have a good reason to arrest all of the officials connected with this concern" (Sovereignty Commission 2-20-2-34-2-1-1). Ash stated that the officers were "in cooperation with COFO which has an office at 100 Rust College Avenue in a building which Rust College has, for many years, used for Rust College purposes" (Sovereignty Commission 2-20-2-34-2-1-1). Correspondence between Zinj Enterprises and the secretary of state noted that "the acknowledgment to the papers of Articles of Incorporation of Zinj Enterprises was acknowledged by Hazel L. Foster, Negro, female, whose residence is Ripley, Mississippi, and who is not authorized to take acknowledgments for any concern proposing to form a corporation in another county, as I understand the law" (Sovereignty Commission 2-20-2-34-2-1-1).

Scarbrough looked through the company files and discovered that in "the correspondence of all the documents concerning this corporation," there was a copy of two receipts, both numbered 200, and the "photostatic copy of the check for $100.00 which is made out to Zinj Enterprises and is countersigned by Eddie L. Smith, Vice President, C.A. Williams, President, and W. B. Mitchell, Treasurer" (Sovereignty Commission 2-20-2-34-2-1-1). The receipt indicated "that perhaps some stock has already been sold as the photostatic copy of the check indicates this concern has a bank account in the Bank of Holly Springs, Holly Springs, Mississippi" (Sovereignty Commission 2-20-2-34-2-1-1). The note, from the photostatic copy of a letter to the secretary of state, dated October 24, 1964, requested that the secretary of state send complete information about the qualifications and registration requirements of stock certificates, and a copy of the Mississippi Securities Act. On October 30, 1964, the Honarable Ben Hawkins, Deputy Secretary of State, answered the inquiry of W. B. Mitchell, Acting Manager and Treasurer for Zinj Enterprises.

Scarbrough concluded that Zinj Enterprises, Inc. had not complied with the Securities Act of the State, advertising in the county paper the intention of the business, or filed for a charter to do business in the state. The state filing system ensured the control of business that did not abide by segregationist policies. Requirements of separate entrances and separate facilities were observed, and as such, a business operating in the state was liable for not taking the proper measures to ensure the continuation of the system.   Second, the state filing system served as catalog of the whereabouts of businesses and individuals in the state which the Commission needed to investigate. Whites were angered that blacks would do something without them for the first time in the town, especially using their own money to finance black commerce.

Zinj proposed to sell $75,000 worth of stocks to only blacks, which Scarbrough believed "will get nowhere in selling $75,000 worth of stock to Mississippi Negroes, but it is possible that the bulk of the common and preferred stock might be sold to some concern with strong civil rights connections in New York or elsewhere" (Sovereignty Commission 2-20-2-34-2-1-1). The intent of Zinj captures a shift in ideology from conservatism to radicalism. Not only were all officers black, but the stock was sold to blacks. The investigator kept a close eye on Zinj, but the company is never mentioned in any of the Sovereignty Commission records after the initial investigation. The company served as mechanism for the support of the boycott that was about to take place after the passage of the Civil Rights Act in 1964. The goal was to set up an organization that aided all those that would suffer from the backlash of participating in the boycott, especially anyone that relied on whites for employment.

The Boycott

Marshall County's boycott had been a carefully planned strategy, orchestrated by local people, mainly Skip Robinson and Eddie Lee Smith, Jr. They organized it from the COFO House at Rust College. COFO had recently rented two buildings near Rust, in addition to the one they had at 100 Rust Avenue. They brought eight telephones in the two additional buildings. Scarbrough anticipated the plan. He believed that "this crew has moved into Marshall County for the purpose of putting on a very large demonstration in Negro voter registration. It is my thinking that this will take place on a similar scale as is now taking place at Selma, Alabama" (Sovereignty Commission 2-20-2-37-1-1-1). The plan that was going to be used in Holly Springs was implemented in Selma after widespread demonstrations in the Alabama town (Cooper and Terrill, 1991). At the time, COFO had been very active in the Holly Springs area and had success in carrying on a boycott against the segregated school at Ashland, in Benton County, only a few miles away. The local black leadership asked COFO for guidance in conducting the boycott. The issue confronting local blacks was how far to act on the boycott.

With the groundwork laid, the plan went public in 1965. On March 13, Eddie Lee Smith, on behalf of the Marshall County Citizens for Progress, presented a petition to the mayor of the City of Holly Springs. Inspired by the Declaration of Independence, the petitioners claimed their rights taken from them "since 1776." "Whites has for a hundred years been able to maintain a ruthless system of social, economic, and physical tyranny and exploitation over the Negro citizens of Holly Springs," read the petition (March 13, 1965, Petition to the City of Holly Springs, Rust College Archives). The protesters demanded immediate change, and equal protection under the law. They based their demands on ten years of "foot-dragging" by the authorities after the Brown decision. Seven of the twelve demands related to children and their well-being, the school, library, and recreational facilities. Among these were the revision of the city school board, that was not an elected body. Also, new appointments of blacks approved by the black leadership had to occur. The second school demand was the total integration of the public schools "in compliance with the letter and the spirit of the 1954 Supreme Court decision in *Brown vs. Board of Education* and with Title IV of the Civil Rights Act of 1964" (March 13, 1965, Petition, Rust College Archives). Along with the desegregation of the schools, the Citizens for Progress asked for better trained teachers and teaching materials. The petition called for integration in spirit, as well as de facto in all public facilities. The three places the mayor was ordered to desegregate by the petitioners were the tax supported public facilities, including the three federally funded housing projects, and the restaurants and service station washrooms, as specified in Title II of the Civil Rights Act of 1964. Finally, the third demand was the removal of the "White" and "Colored" signs in the Marshall County Courthouse. Highway 7 was the next problem of concern. It was the main thoroughfare and was usually congested with lumber and cotton trucks, and crossed in front of Rust College, the segregated school, and the playground. The Citizens for Progress asked for traffic lights and police help during times children arrived and left school. They were also concerned that city facilities like the pool and the one community gym, which was located in the white high school, were still segregated. The city decided to deal with the integration of the pool by filling it with dirt the day after several black children tried to swim in it.

The strategy for winning the boycott were laid out in goals and objectives that blacks could rally around. First, the desegregation of businesses in the square through the removal of "Colored" signs. Second, the desegregation of the courthouse and all public buildings, including the library and the pool, with the removal of similar signs. Third, the improvement of the infrastructure in the black section of town through the posting of speed limits and traffic lights. Finally, the last section, the largest, focused on the desegregation of schools and the job security of black teachers. In closing, the petition declared to Mayor Coopwood, by name, "what is your answer. . . . You know in your heart that we are right when we sing 'We'll Never Turn Back.' What will you do?" (March 13, 1965, Petition, Rust College Archives). In 1999, one of the boycott leaders, Eddie Smith, now the mayor, recalled how the leaders went about implementing the boycott. Correctly, he saw black unity as crucial for success. Smith remembered:

> . . . when I came back . . . in nineteen sixty-four, and he and I [Skip] did talk . . . about what he and I needed to do, to get people involved . . . and you know you have to get involved, but you really didn't have the masses involved . . . so we started brainstorming what we should use . . . and what happened was, I took three pictures . . . that I though everybody in the community could relate to . . . there was no blacks in police corps in city hall . . . we had no blacks on the school board in city hall. . . .
>
> . . . and the traffic lights on the interstate between the Rust College . . . and I was amazed at it and at this time there was more walking, us kids walked to school . . . over to the school, so there was a lot pedestrian traffic and those trucks would just come zoom, you know . . . so it was kind of dangerous, and so we approached the issue . . . it came through the city council, to deal with that . . . well, what it did, we had a bunch of people out here, school teachers . . . a bunch of people, even the representative of MI . . . so it was just like, so this is what you should do . . . they been told two or three times and this is going into nineteen-sixty-five and they did not respond and so we organized the first year march that was locally motivated, the COFO and Rust students had been doing . . . and we made demands on that . . . this is a petition that was . . . you can keep that . . . that was sensible and then by the time we got up there, we had everybody put in all the other things in the picture . . . demands that had been put in, you know, much more than had been put in originally . . . so they wouldn't respond, so then the next thing we did was we came back and this was the second march when we come back to get an answer . . . that's what this is about . . . that's when talked and we out-smarted

them, because we had information . . . and five minutes before we met . . . and we planned the black leadership to sit down . . . and we're not going to leave this you know . . . and where I was born at the time . . . we'll march anyway, but we just wont do it in the square, and we had printed up a banner. . . .

Well, see what happened was they had the police, the state troopers down there in front of the courthouse . . . a bunch of reporters . . . they weren't going to beat us up, those state troopers, we just marched right around them to the church . . . and we found out they closed the building . . . and blacks . . . you'll find some of that, in the municipal courthouse record . . . when they got an injunction against us.

Smith planned the event for the media, in case Holly Springs made national headlines. Smith remembered returning and organizing the boycott. His major problem was the disorganization of the black community. In order to rally the black community, Smith and Robinson devised specific symbols of white misconduct to protest. He also emphasized the need for the boycott to be local. Smith understood that to execute boycott he had to outsmart the white establishment by protesting peacefully, and relying on strategies such as media coverage to win out.

Unfortunately, changes were slow. As the school year progressed, changes did not come to the school system, but the business establishments began to slowly make concessions. Black buying power was immense and evident in Holly Springs. Blacks composed over 70 percent of the county's population. In the summertime, the Citizens for Progress decided to continue their quest for school integration with a second petition for the sole purpose of change in the school systems of Marshall County and Holly Springs. In July 1965, the boycott campaign took a harder term. That month the leadership addressed the various governing bodies of the whole county with demands for change by addressing the Marshall County Board of Supervisors, Marshall County Board of Education, Holly Springs Board of Aldermen, Holly Springs Board of Education, and the Marshall County Human Relations Committee. Smith stated that after four years of trying, the black community of Holly Springs and Marshall County were fed up with whites' legal attempts to deny change (Follow-up letter to March 13, 1965, Petition, Rust College Archives). The two demands leveled at the Board of Education of Marshall County and Holly Springs centered on their violations of Title I compliance. The School Board had used the shortage of school funds in Marshall County as a pretense for keeping the status quo. The petitioners reminded the school board that the U.S. Office of Education offered financial aid to counties that could not afford a unified school system, and could not pay for equal salaries and expenses as required under Titles IV and VII of the Civil Rights Act through the Department of Health, Education, and Welfare (HEW) (Rust College Archives).

The July follow-up letter raised a second issue: the county's refusal to negotiate "fair" contracts with janitors and teachers. The Citizens for Progress's attack focused on the superintendent's claim of shortage of funds needed for integration and change; a claim that appeared several times in the *South Reporter*. However, if the city complied with the U.S. Office of Education's decree of integration, Title I funds would be immediately received by the city (Rust College Archives). The problem for the city was in the requirements set by the federal government for desegregated schools, and in the stipulation for equal salary for all individuals, without racial discrimination.

Initially, the boycott succeeded, and white businesses were panicked. They sought resolution in part trough the formation of a community action committee. Smith and the Citizens for Progress attacked the committee, under the leadership of the Marshall County Board of Supervisors. The Marshall County Board of Supervisors had set up this committee in 1964 to oversee the implementation of the Civil Rights Act of 1964 and to look at the possibilities of disbursing federal monies allotted for public institutions that were abiding by federal desegregation laws. The Board of Supervisors' committee was a bi-racial token committee designed to keep everybody happy and give the veneer of change. The federal programs that the committee had to explore were of greatest benefit to the black population of Marshall County and Holly Springs. The committee had never met. In not meeting, the committee had kept the federal programs from being enacted in the county and punished the black community for the boycott. Spurred by the action of the boycott, the Temporary Marshall County Community Action Committee was finally set up to propose a plan passed unanimously by the County Board of Supervisors on the make-up of the committee in February 1966. The committee's role was to oversee the integration of the public facilities. The appointment of more conservative blacks, whose support was vital to the success of the boycott, was an attempt to quell the boycott. Committees, like this one in Marshall County, were ordered into existence by the federal government, under the Civil Rights Act of 1964, to eventually determine that the distribution of money be equally represented by both races.

The July complaint from the boycotters was regarding who would make up the committee. There was a split in the Holly Springs black community, as in other black communities in the South, on the basis of social class and involvement within the movement (Dittmer, 1995). The main objective of the committee was to release federal monies for summer programs, but federal programs could not be administered in segregated counties or cities. Thus, in Marshall County by not integrating the county facilities, the committee did not have to meet. The Citizens for Progress believed that by influencing the Board of Supervisors they could cause change within the committee. Also, just receiving the concession of controlling the appointment of members in the committee was a moral victory, especially since it would reinforce the importance of the power behind the boycott.

In the past, whites chose the black representation. Blacks chosen were reliant on the white community for a living. They were also regarded as accommodationist by the black community. For example, appointing the principal of the black schools allowed whites to dictate the Committee's actions since contracts were given year-to-year and depended on the individuals signing a loyalty oath. Second, St. Mary's School was to send a representative, and its student base came from black professionals connected with MI, who did not support the movement. David Caldwell, local black business owner, remembers the senseless arguing over the Committee, which led to the boycott losing its effectiveness.

The Citizens for Progress submitted an alternative plan for the appointments of representatives to the Committee. They believed that the fifteen black representatives should be constituted as follows: (1) One each from the NAACP, MI College, the Black Credit Union, Farm Bureau, Cedar Grove Mason Lodge, the President of the Sims Parent Teacher Association (PTA), and (2) from each of the five districts that the County was divided into. Each district would send two representatives, for a total of ten. The Citizens for Progress raised an issue of contention by using the five districts as centers of representation because it would mean that Holly Springs would be overrepresented and the county underrepresented. Another issue raised by the black community was that the new proposed plan only included one representative from W.T. Sims High School and none from the county schools. Eddie Lee Smith also saw W.T. Sims as crucial. However, Skip Robinson, who was from Potts Camp in the county, did not see eye to eye with Smith on this issue. The split would become more apparent in the later years of the Movement. In the end, the black representatives came from the original proposal, and the Citizens' proposal was rejected.

The businesses believed they had abided by the demands set forth by the Citizens for Progress. Businessmen believed that they had completed their part of the agreement. The matter had been corrected because the merchants took a large hit in the pocket and began to cave to the demands. The focus on the representation of the Committee allowed the white business owners to regroup and use racketeering laws to sue blacks involved in boycotts in 1965 and 1966. They cited that it was a result of their dissatisfaction with the enforcement of the Civil Rights Act of 1964 and Voting Rights Act of 1965 (Injunction, Marshall County Chancery Court, Suit No. 10,689, August 5, 1966). The suit named everyone associated with the boycott. The suit listed forty names. The August injunction prohibited any interference with prospective customers who were patronizing the various stores in Holly Springs. It was brought by twenty-six Holly Springs businessmen against the officers of the Marshall County Citizens for Progress, and against thirty other residents in the lawsuit. The boycott prevented blacks from trading with the various stores around the square in Holly Springs and elsewhere in the city that were segregated. The year-long boycott was revived by the argument over control of the Marshall County Board of Supervisors. Robinson and Smith had been arguing about when to end the boycott. The injunction did not lead to anything since by the time it was signed, businesses on the square had begun to remove Jim Crow obstacles for blacks. The boycott was successful, as Smith remembers, because of its ability to rally local blacks around attainable goals. Smith recalls that:

> in order to be a member of the NAACP, you had to come up with a movement that people would recognize that was not illegal and that's kind of where Skip and I split, at that point, but luckily we were running together you know slow the movement and we had to go back just to show them that we weren't beat . . . and do the boycott . . and then we went back and did that . . . boycotts . . . and we got things done . . . and deal with some issues . . . and so I, at that point left. . . .

If the Community Action Committee represented a victory for the protesters in February, August events reversed that success. At that time, Judge William H. Anderson issued an injunction against the boycotters, which effectively ended the boycott. Judge William H. Anderson handed down an injunction on August 5, 1966, against the Citizens for Progress to stop picketing and boycotting business, effectively ending the one-year boycott (Marshall County Chancery Court, Suit No. 10,869). The injunction called for a temporary restraining order and a fine of $2,000 to be divided among the defendants and paid to the plaintiffs (Chancery Court, Suit No. 10,869). About the same time, the Sovereignty Commission appeared on the scene again. On August 10, 1966, at the request of Senator George Yarbrough, Scarbrough came to Holly Springs to determine whether the Commission could be of any help in the demonstrations and boycotts which had been going on in Holly Springs for several days since the court order to cease (Sovereignty Commission 2-20-2-74-1-1-1).

Whites accused the Citizens for Progress of intimidating witnesses, including influencing several blacks to swear that they had been threatened by members of the Marshall County Citizens for Progress when they attempted to not boycott. That evidence, obtained in depositions and petitions, as well as statements by various merchants, was held to be sufficient to justify Judge William Anderson handing down an injunction against the boycott. The final arguments made were that the pickets were marching around the square in Holly Springs displaying various placards making demands upon the city over which the merchants had no control whatsoever. A lasting effect of the boycott was a loss of economic power, the only real power blacks held. The white-owned stores in the square had more selection and prices than the local black stores, according to local blacks. Holly Springs had about 100 black-owned businesses before 1965, a number that dwindled to about thirty in one year. The remaining businesses were the traditional black operations: garages, beauty shops, mechanics, music stores, pool halls, package stores, and juke joints (music halls). Thus, in an ironic twist of fate, the only real power that blacks possessed, economic independence, was done in by their successful boycott of the businesses. Local blacks began to shop in the white-owned stores, proving that economics was more powerful than ideology. Smith and Robinson had relied on local blacks to believe in the long term goals of the Movement, yet they could not harness black economic power when blacks acted in their interests rather than those of the Movement.

The original intent of the Citizens for Progress was to end segregation not only in businesses but in public facilities. Without political power, only black economic power could succeed in this action. White businesses gave in rather quickly but the local government held on. With no political power, i.e., votes, the city and county remained segregated. In the end, the businesses, backed by the local government, pushed for an end to the boycott. Losing this battle was not a major setback for the Movement. Boycotts would never again work in Marshall County as Skip Robinson experienced in 1969 and 1974 in Byhalia.

The local movement had made its most visible effort to end desegregation in the boycott of 1965. The results were not what they expected. They gained access to businesses on the square. Their immense economic power, which came from their large numbers, had forced businesses to remove "Colored" signs and segregated counters from their establishments. However, years of tradition were still too powerful to change. In accomplishing its other aims, the boycott failed to cause any change in schools or in the public buildings on the square. As for the schools, it would take another five years for desegregation to be enforced by court order in 1970. The boycott also was the last local effort to desegregate the community. After 1966, the federal government became more involved in its efforts to force desegregation in the South. One such effort became Freedom of Choice, allowing blacks to attend any school in the county.

CHAPTER SIX

Civil Rights: The Effects
of the Boycott and the Civil Rights Act, 1966–1972

Introduction

The collapse of the boycott in the summer of 1966 marked a double watershed in the history of Holly Springs' black activism. It represented, first, the end of localism and local initiative. Just so, it marked a new era of federal intervention. At the same time, the six-year period after the boycott represented the black effort, largely unsuccessful, to capitalize on elected politics. This chapter deals with the succession of black political activism in Holly Springs, focusing on the attempts to register blacks.

The act of registering to vote is an example of the lack of retaliation from the white community. One important aspect is the presence of the federal government, which along with the ability of blacks to register, and consequently to run for office, led to a change in the political landscape of 1966 and 1967. That change was short-lived as blacks lost in every single race they entered. It is not until 1972 that a black candidate was elected in a biracial contest in Mississippi (State of Mississippi Report, 1968–1972). The results were not as intended for blacks. The power structure remained unchanged, but as of 1968, black votes and candidates had to be taken seriously.

Voter Registration and Elections

After the Mississippi Summer, voter registration had gone at a slow pace. The Sovereignty Commission's Tom Scarbrough, for example, kept a careful chronicle of the lack of process. On October 19, 1965, Scarbrough, visited a number of North Mississippi counties, among them Marshall and Benton, in search for any "subversive activities or civil rights or any other group who might be inclined to circumvent normal law channels" (Sovereignty Commission 10-57-0-28-1-1-1). In neighboring Benton County, Scarbrough contacted Sheriff Brook Ward, Circuit Clerk Lawson Mathis, Superintendent of Education J. D. Bennett, an attorney for the school board, Haymon McKenzie, who was also employed by the Marshall County School Board. While he discovered two federal registrars working behind the post office, he also noted that Benton County officials agreed "that the federal authorities have not been too successful in registering very many Negroes in the county as yet" (Sovereignty Commission 10-57-0-28-1-1-1). According to the City Clerk, Sandra Young, even today they have trouble approaching blacks about filling out forms and U.S. Census information because of their mistrust.

Since 1965, there had been "4,016 Negroes registered and only 1,069 Whites" in Marshall County (Sovereignty Commission 8-19-2-25-2-1-1). For Scarbrough, the "Negroes will out vote the whites in Marshall County" (Sovereignty Commission 8-19-2-25-2-1-1). Skip Robinson had made a speech to a group of blacks during a Head Start meeting on behalf of "Negroes running for U.S. Senate etc. and at this meeting stated he was running for sheriff in Marshall county next year" (Sovereignty Commission 8-19-2-25-2-1-1). Mayor Coopwood predicted that "Negroes will run for almost every office and is afraid they are organized so well, some will be elected" (Sovereignty Commission 8-19-2-25-2-1-1). Mayor Coopwood's fear soon materialized, if not fully, as in 1965 and 1966, blacks began running for office. The candidacy of blacks had its genesis in 1964 as individual blacks had decided that they should be politically visible. Before the issue of what occurred after the announcement of black candidates' intentions to run for office, the year-long boycott of 1965 established the black voice as a viable political group that had to be respected.

Scarbrough understood that the local movement could snowball into a popular protest, and that is why he tried to help local clerks stop black voter registration. For example, Scarbrough spoke with the Circuit Clerk, Otis Clayton, and informed him the way other clerks forestalled during registration drives by the NAACP, CORE, and "other agitative groups." He was pleased to learn that the Justice Department demanded nothing from Otis Clayton's registration records. He also noted that clerks of both Benton and Union counties had not been so lucky. The Justice Department had subpoenaed the records of both. He instructed Clayton further that request and advised that clerks had refused the Justice Department's request and insisted "that they [county clerks] would have to have a court order to inspect their records" (Sovereignty Commission 8-19-2-25-2-1-1). That action by the federal government was an attempt to aid local blacks, who had not trusted the federal government because before the Civil Rights Act of 1964, they had followed a policy of nonprotection and noninterference with local affairs (Carson, 1981, pp. 34-39).

Even though black registration remained low, various factors encouraged individual blacks to seek office in the sixties. For one thing, the Movement had awakened the spirit in individual black leaders to seize the brass ring of political office. For, even with black registration low, the huge racial majority (70%:30%) suggested fewer blacks had to register to elect their own. And finally, the numbers of whites seeking office especially for sheriff, where eight white men and two black men had qualified as candidates for sheriff in the Democratic primary. Whites feared that blacks would wind up as winners for the runoff for sheriff "since there are eight whites to split the vote" (Sovereignty Commission 2-20-2-59-1-1-1). In a secret meeting with Senator Yarbrough, his brother, the editor of the *South Reporter,* and Sheriff Ash, Scarbrough advised them that they should "very quietly qualify someone as an independent to run in the November election if the need arises for every office in the county which is being contested by other races" (Sovereignty Commission 2-20-2-59-1-1-1).

All these elements appeared in Marshall County by 1966 in the particular sensitive race for sheriff and chancery clerk, where Clifton R. Whitley, a former candidate for the U.S. Senate against Jim Eastland, ran against the incumbent, and former Sheriff Flick Ash. The chancery clerk office was the most contested office in the county because the annual salary was based on a percentage of the total amount of property taxes collected. Black candidates, Oscar L. Fant ran for Circuit Clerk, James V. Murdock, Charley Polk, and McEwen Walker ran for District Supervisors. Marshall County was divided into four districts. District Supervisor positions were highly contested because of the power that they carried. Another black candidate, Osborne Bell, ran for coroner. He would later become the first black sheriff in the history of Marshall County in 1980. He died after being shot on duty in 1986.

On March 2, 1967, the first black to ever qualify for the Democratic primary ran for the office of supervisor in District One. Two weeks later, Oscar Fant announced his candidacy for circuit clerk of Marshall County, becoming the second black to qualify for the formerly all-white Democratic primary. The next week incumbent Leslie R. Tomlinson beat black candidate William Sidney Payne in a runoff. The runoff produced the largest turnout ever in the county for an election. Tomlinson won by a margin of 358, showing once again that local blacks did not have enough registered voters in the county although they made up 70 percent of the population.

Even as the boycott collapsed in the summer of 1966, more blacks were registering to vote and becoming active in politics. In August 1966, before the primary, two more civil rights leaders ran for office; Quentell Gipson for County Superintendent of Education and Lannie Cummings, Jr., for Sheriff and Tax Collector. In a surprise, Quentell Gipson almost won by collecting all the black votes. He and four other blacks gathered enough votes in the primary to be in runoff elections. In the runoff, when all voters voted along racial lines, they all lost. The focus on local politics became the main concern of the blacks. The local population blamed the black awakening on the federal government as it provided an easy target for local politicians.

On January 15, 1970, Senator John Stennis addressed a group at an Oxford, Mississippi, meeting where he stated that "the South is being imposed on while other areas of the country are neglected" (*South Reporter*, January 16, 1970). The same week, a letter sent to the newspaper by 300 taxpayers claimed that they were angry about the federal government control of their communities. This letter is significant since it places the blame of racial relations and schooling on the national government. The belief in local schools was strong in the small communities who took pride in the "Separate Schools Systems" (Wolters, 1984). During this time, most attacks were verbal. Politeness ruled. In discussing this issue, the lack of any Ku Klux Klan demonstrations, or anti-black violence reveals the nature of the town. Also, the difference in a movement initiated by locals is treated as not threatening, whereas the federal government is seen as destroying the community. The difficulty in causing change lies in the closeness and politeness of blacks and whites. The nature of desegregation is even more bizarre. The Freedom of Choice students reported no physical violence, or gang attacks by whites, or segregation within the school toward them. They were taken more aback by the treatment of their own fellow black students at the black high school, W.T. Sims. One last act of the federal government dealt with the issue of elections. On February 12, 1970, the U.S. Attorney ordered the redistricting of Marshall County to have five districts, each with an equal population, valuation and each a village (within a 5 percent margin). Holly Springs was in districts 1, 2, 3, 4, and 5. The new redistricting gave the city, one white, two black, and one 50/50 district for elections and referendums, as well as for aldermen. One major problem for blacks was that they split their votes among several black candidates, thereby leaving the white candidate as the winner.

As blacks began to achieve political visibility, they began to use U.S. courts to challenge traditional practice. One instance occurred in 1972, seven years after the widespread registration of blacks in Marshall County. Rust and MI College students sued Marshall County over the vague residency status needed to register to vote. They requested an injunction against Circuit Clerk Edwin Callicutt, Jr., who they stated had prevented them from registering. Although more blacks were running for public office, city and county officials were still resisting the registration of blacks. Callicutt had been advised to stop blacks from registering to vote by the Sovereignty Commission. In Marshall County and Jackson, the presence of a black middle class, and black colleges that supported them, allowed locals the freedom to use the courts and legislation to fight for their civil rights. Other parts of the state did not possess that advantage, which led to violence early on in the struggle.

On April 12, 1973, the *South Reporter* reported that a suit was filed by the Justice Department in Oxford against Marshall County for not allowing black students from Rust to register in the May 8, 1972, primary. The same suit was originally filed on January 20, 1973, and included allegations that whites were illegally registered in 1971 by Circuit Clerk Edwin Callicutt, City Clerk W. W. Newsom, and the Marshall County Board of Elections Commissions. Blacks accused officials of illegally rejecting the applications of forty-seven black students between June 30, 1972, and January 20, 1973.

The lawsuit overshadowed the theater burning down in 1973. The theater had been closed and reopened on two occasions. It was a major source of tension because it had remained segregated. The fight to integrate the theater began in 1961 with a letter addressed to Leon Roundtree, the theater's owner. Rust College students took the role of leadership in integrating the theater. The seating arrangement in the theater was such that blacks sat in the balcony after buying their tickets from the booth to the right of the theater, and whites sat on the ground level after buying their tickets from the left-side box office. The theater had been closed in the mid1960s when two mixed couples had tried to buy tickets. The first couple, a white man and a black woman, both from COFO, attempted to sit in the ground section. A second couple, a black man and a white woman, also from COFO, attempted to sit at the balcony. They were both turned away from the theater, and Roundtree decided to close the theater. The theater had been the only form of entertainment in town, and had been very selective in its showings, as all southern theaters had been, careful not to show any movies that "preached" racial equality.

On Friday, August 2, 1974, almost a year after the suit against the Board of Elections was filed, Chancery Judge William H. Anderson granted an injunction against the United League of Marshall County and Skip Robinson for their boycott of Byhalia, ending the short boycott in northwest Marshall County. After ten years, the people of Marshall were tired of the Civil Rights Movement. It just faded out. The Movement was done in by token public offices given to influential blacks, a new welfare program, a vocational high school, and the slow migration of whites from the public schools to Marshall Academy (MA). The political struggle that began in 1960 had become by 1974, old and tired. Many of the leaders left Marshall County, and the new leaders could not sustain the Movement. They also became victims of widespread poverty in the late 1960s, the closing of MI College, and the demise of Rust, which had only about 800 students and no longer possessed the influence after white state schools were opened to blacks. Rust was not any different than most black colleges and universities. By the end of the decade more blacks were in integrated state schools than in black institutions (Fleming, Gill, and Swinton, 1978). Skip Robinson and Henry Boyd could not muster the support that the Movement had in the mid-1960s, although everyone in town respected them. The following section deals with schools and the Civil Rights Movement, and the battle for desegregation, a pyrrhic victory that in the end cost the resegregation of the community.

CHAPTER SEVEN

Desegregation and the Public Schools, 1966–1970

Introduction

Freedom of Choice governed schools between 1966 and 1970. Before 1966, Marshall County and Holly Springs schools remained strictly segregated. Under pressure from the federal government, however, some form of integration became unavoidable. While some school districts chose Massive Resistance, as had Prince Edward County, Virginia, closing schools before racially integrating them; Marshall County and Holly Springs resorted to the Freedom of Choice plan. Freedom of Choice allowed all students to attend the school they wanted. In Marshall County, grades one, two, seven and twelve were opened to Freedom of Choice. Each school district across Mississippi had the right to choose how to integrate the schools. Freedom of Choice was safe in Marshall because it followed court decisions. Integration of schools occurred in two phases. Freedom of Choice was the first phase lasting less than five years. It powerfully affected the local population. The refusal of local districts to integrate forced the U.S. Courts to take action, thereby, beginning the second phase integration: desegregation. This phase was fought in the U.S. District Courts. By 1968, the South was faced with multiple class action suits against the schools for violation of the civil rights of black children. One such case was *Clarence Anthony vs. Marshall County and Holly Springs Schools*. The plaintiffs won as the U.S. Court ruled that Freedom of Choice had not desegregated the schools. The Court gave the schools the option to use testing to assign children to each grade based on their score. U.S. Senators from Mississippi advocated that the court ruling violated the Civil Rights Act because they favored blacks over whites. The state used money to support their students who wanted to attend private schools. Finally, the local school districts attempted delay tactics to keep schools segregated. In the end, they failed as the federal courts and Justice Hugo Black ushered in the end of Freedom of Choice and token integration with a plan for total desegregation of the schools in 1970. After lengthy delays in integration, the U.S. Courts forced schools to desegregate by February 1, 1970.

Freedom of Choice, 1967–1969

Marshall County determined to now integrate in four grades. For various reasons few chose integration. While the legal and sociological history of this phase of integration has its own report, the personal and intimate history is worth telling too. It also possessed its own sociological implications. *The South Reporter* discouraged blacks from sending their children to the white schools during the Freedom of Choice period. At Holly Springs High School, Ruth Greer, Al Beck, and Modina Reynolds entered the twelfth grade. In an angry letter to the paper, the black leadership attacked Freedom of Choice and the paper which urged blacks to keep their children in their own schools. "Remember that the editor of this paper is a white Southerner. We doubt that he has ever set foot in Frazier or Sims," appeared in the opening paragraph (Rust College Archives).

The most popular course at Sims was clerical skills, yet the school possessed few typewriters, little lab equipment for Chemistry or Biology, no new library books in over ten years, no football field or basketball gym, or industrial arts shop. Angry, Sims students followed several leaders for a one week sit-in at Holly High, the only major incident by the black student body of Sims. The schools in Holly Springs were only integrating grades one, two, seven, and twelve. In total, twenty students took advantage of the situation. Freedom of Choice in the early grades was unencumbered by the authorities as the town did not want to be compared to Selma, Grenada, or Prince Edward County, where mobs attacked young school children for integrating the schools (Wolters, 1984). Third, the "lower class element" that made up the foot soldiers of such attacks on Freedom of Choicers lived in the outer edges of the county, outside of the city limits. Fourth, Holly Springs was heavily dependent on outside industry, such as CocaCola, for their economy. The city could not and would not risk a race riot, especially if smaller children were attacked. At the seventh grade level, only two boys entered school, and their family name and position was such that they were not harassed. The five that entered high schools were virtually invisible to anyone but their friends at Sims or their new classmates at Holly High. The Holly High Tiger Yearbook placed all five of their pictures on a separate page at the end of the senior section so that it could be removed if any of the students did not want blacks in their yearbook (1966–1967 Holly Springs High School Yearbook). The year went along smoothly at the high school, except for the personal battles of each student who chose to attend the formerly all-white high school.

As 1968 approached, court dockets overflowed across the state and the South, as a new generation of challenges to the Brown I and II decisions on school integration arose. For blacks in Holly Springs, the year held great promise, but, as the school year came to a close, a more conservative president came to Rust, thus ending the unwavering support for civil rights by the college. On May 30, 1968, during commencement, President W.A. McMillan was inaugurated at Rust. Eddie Smith, the vocal leader in the 1965 economic boycott, had all but left the college, and Skip Robinson had left the Civil Rights Movement for the Nation of Islam. The third leader of the Movement, Henry Boyd, Jr., who ran the Freedom School in 1964, began to concentrate on his job as a teacher.

In June 1968, Nat Brooks, the athletic trainer for Holly High football since 1918, was honored for his loyalty in a ceremony. This event was a metaphor for the conflict between the old living with the new changes that were about to come. The event to honor Nat Brooks for his loyalty marked whites' perception of white-black relationships in the South. During homecoming, Nat was allowed to run across the football field collecting $100 bills pinned to clotheslines every ten yards as the frenzied white crowd cheered him on. This, of course, occurred after the pep squad along with the football team traveled to Nat's shack on Center Street and picked him up, placed him in a convertible, and put him in the parade to the high school, where he ran into the field for his money.

Freedom of Choice and Desegregation: Phase Two

If few students and families chose integration in phase one, phase two saw a marked increase in integration and black interest in white schools. As a result of school desegregation, and federal legislation passed in 1968, 356 blacks applied for Freedom of Choice for the September 1969 school year in both the city and county. The forms were filed on May 15, 1969, and announced in the front page of the *South Reporter*. The following is the breakdown of those who would attend the Holly Springs schools:

Grade	Number	Grade	Number
6	5	10	28
8	36	11	23
9	24	12	17

In June, two more events took place in Holly Springs that signaled a shift in both schooling and the power structure of the black leadership. Eddie L. Smith took out an ad in the newspaper for candidacy for the school board, a position he would win, becoming the first black elected to office in the county. This would lead to his separation from the Movement in the city and his push for desegregation in the county. The focus of the effort for the county, and the relative lack of power of county whites, led to more desegregation in county schools and facilities as opposed to the city. In the same month, St. Mary's senior class graduated. This was an uneventful situation, except that the school was all black. The closing of the white St. Joseph and black St. Mary's, and the new desegregated school, CADET, provided a preview of what would occur in the public schools. The whites left either for the still segregated public schools or for the newly established Marshall Academy.

As the court cases loomed over the schools, Marshall County and Holly Springs decided to use alternate plans for integration. In phase two, testing replaced Freedom of Choice as the tool for integration. On June 12, 1969, county and city school districts released their plans to integrate the schools through the use of achievement scores. The U.S. courts had ordered several school districts in Mississippi to find an alternative to Freedom of Choice. Marshall County and Holly Springs schools chose to use achievement scores because whites scored higher than blacks. The school board would test the first three grades, and the students with the highest scores would be assigned to each school pending space, first to the white school, Sallie Cochran, and then to the black school, Frazier. Then, for the next three years, three more grades would be tested per year, 4 through 6 in 1970, 7 through 9 in 1971, and 10 through 12 in 1972, until all grades were tested and the four year plan completed. The Fifth District Court offered a counter proposal; all children would be tested in the spring of 1970 and reassigned to their new schools. The district court gave attorneys until January 16, 1970, to file objections to the desegregation plan, and a hearing was scheduled for January 30.

In 1968, Clarence Anthony filed a class action lawsuit against the Marshall County and Holly Springs school districts in order to desegregate both school districts. U.S. District Chief Justice William Keady found against the plaintiffs, and in favor of Freedom of Choice. Anthony appealed to the Fifth Circuit Court. Based on the evidence that forty-three out of 5,574 black children in both districts had attended white schools, and that not one single white child had attended black schools, Judge Ainsworth ruled that a new plan had to be formulated by the school districts (Mississippi No. 56432, US 409 F.2d 1282, 1969). Ainsworth cited other cases such as *Bowman v. County School Board of Charles City County* (US 382 F.2d 326, 333, 1967), where the judiciary mandated a plan for creating a "unitary, nonracial system." He also referred to *Green v. County School Board of New Kent County* (US 430, 88 S.Ct. 1689, 20 L.Ed.2d 716, 1968), as an example of segregation continuing under freedom of choice because of outside influence on the schools. On June 19, 1969, the plaintiffs proposed a competing plan. Unlike the Marshall County plan, the new plan proposed testing all 12 grades. The scores on the test would determine the school students would attend the following year. Based on the scores of the previous year, the plaintiffs predicted that the school breakdown would fall as Table 7.1 illustrates.

After hearing both sides, on July 17, 1969, federal judge Keady approved this schemes in order to insure integration with the test scores for grades one through four, and that 20 percent of the students in grades 11 and 12 of the formerly white schools would be black. He also mandated one black teacher for every six white teachers in white schools, and one white teacher for every six black teachers in black schools. He demanded that school facilities be integrated by 1970. Testing was a means of keeping the black students out, while complying with Brown II. Judge Keady warned that "if testing did not produce substantial desegregation, the plan would be ruled unconstitutional" (Mississippi No. 26432, US 409 F.2d 1287, 1969).

Following the judge's order, the *South Reporter* printed an advertisement for the parents of Marshall County students for the dates of the school placement tests for children in grades 1 through 4 (August 7, 1969). All children in grades 1 through 4 would attend an orientation program that required a parent to transport them. The session was held one week before the test. Marshall whites had fought integration in the U.S. courts; they continued to resist even when the judiciary opposed them. This mandate to test the children, the school districts decided, they "could not" afford to transport them to the exams. Thus, on August 14, 1969, the U.S. Fifth District Court ordered that the eighty-one highest scoring students in grades 1 through 4 attend Sallie Cochran Elementary, and the rest Frazier. Second, all other grades would accept students by Freedom of Choice, except grades 11 and 12, which in accordance to Judge Keady's ruling had to have a 20 percent black student body for the 1969–1970 school year. However, the U.S. Court added that in the 1970–1971 school year, grades nine through twelve had to have a 20 percent black student body. The U.S. Court also ordered that in 1969–1970 school year, one in six persons at the school had to be of a different race, and with the facility fully desegregated by 1970–1971. Last, the Court forced Holly Springs to provide transportation to all those students who used it the previous year, in order for them to take the test.

Table 7.1 Expected Enrollment of Schools in Holly Springs after Testing, the *South Reporter*

Grade	Whites (Holly High)	Blacks (Holly High)	Whites (Sims)	Blacks (Sims)
1	44	40	16	160
2	39	36	22	164
3	38	33	13	145
4	36	42	18	158
5	43	34	19	141
6	43	30	20	140
7	38	32	17	138
8	36	20	22	151
9	39	17	16	137
10	54	15	15	86
11	63	22	7	97
12	51	11	5	44
Total	524	332	190	1561

While Marshall County still resisted, the school district asked for extra time. At a hearing at Aderdeen, on Friday, September 12, the Holly Springs Municipal Separate School District, Marshall County School District,

Tunica School District, and Sunflower School District requested that federal judge William Keady modify his original order of testing the first four grades. The districts worried about the dropout rate in forcing 20 percent of eleventh and twelfth grades into a different school. The judge refused. He ordered Marshall County and Holly Springs to "persuade" blacks to enter the eleventh and twelfth grades, and ordered grades 1 through 4 to be retested on October 15, 1969. In order to avoid any more delays from parents not testing their children, the Court imposed a penalty of a one-year suspension from any form of schooling, public or private, for any child who did not take the test. And still, whites resisted. Once again, in the face of impending desegregation, and in view of an increase in enrollment, the Mississippi Private School Council (MPSC) asked the state legislature to pass three bills to aid parents of children who attended private schools. The week before, Governor John Bell Williams had passed a threefold package that involved tuition grants, loans, and tax credits for patrons of both secular and religious schools.

In order to combat the impending court decisions, Mississippi Senator Jaime Whitten attempted to pass the Whitten Amendment through the U.S. Congress. As a law, it specified that "no part of the funds contained in this act [Elementary and Secondary Education Act (ESEA)] may be used to force busing of students, the abolishment of schools, or to force any students attending any elementary or secondary school to attend a particular school against the choice of his or her parents." The Elementary and Secondary Education Act had been passed in 1968 to help reform education in the U.S., especially in lower-income areas. Senators Whitten and John Stennis held that favoring blacks over whites violated the law under the Civil Rights Act of 1964, so the ESEA was breaking federal law. Both Whitten and Stennis also concluded that although schools in the South were being attacked for Freedom of Choice, the state of New York practiced the same policy without judicial prejudice. Finally, both Senators argued that States' Rights were being violated by the use of "federal money to force racial integration in schools," while at the same time making references to Reconstruction.

With both the local government and the U.S. senators in the fray, the Sovereignty Commission was not far behind in the effort to forestall desegregation. Investigator Fulton Tutor contacted Superintendent of Education Edward Malliken about using local teachers instead of bringing workers from the Department of Health, Education and Welfare (HEW) of the Office of Education to administer the tests. This suggestion was blocked by the U.S. judge. Tutor also used examples of other counties to instruct the citizens of Marshall. Thus, he noted bomb scares in Aberdeen in Monroe County. He spent September 24 finding someone who could search for the bombs. According to Tutor, "no one really believed there was a bomb but was afraid not to search and see." School was reopened the next day, but Tutor was worried about the "nuisance" of having to close the schools, which could lead to having the students in the streets and a disruption to everyday life (Sovereignty Commission 2-20-2-65-1-1-1).

In October of 1969, the state of Mississippi and its school districts were running out of options to delay the integration of schools. On October 16, 1969, under threat from the federal government to take action against the state, Governor John Bell Williams vetoed a bill that would allow a half credit, up to $50,000 of state income tax donations, to give public, parochial, and all other accredited school children scholarships. Williams had proposed the tuition bill, which was passed overwhelmingly by the House but killed in the Senate. The news reaffirmed the reality of desegregation. Judge Keady mailed the test grades to parents on Monday October 10, and the school assignments on October 13. Table 7.2 shows how each school's population would look for grades 1 through 4 after the test results. Once again, sending whites to the black school was unacceptable to the parents who threatened to keep their children at home if forced to attend the black school. Also, for the first time, blacks would outnumber whites at Sallie Cochran.

Table 7.2 Grade Breakdown for Grades 1–4 after Testing, Holly Springs, the *South Reporter*

Grade	Sallie Cochran (White)	Sallie Cochran (Black)	Frazier (White)	Frazier (Black)
1	44	44	30	100
2	35	46	13	94
3	42	41	5	95
4	37	44	11	114
Total	158	175	59	403

Testing would cause the population of Sallie Cochran to change dramatically if those children with the high scores were allowed into the school. The ploy of the school's attorneys had been practiced in other parts of the state. The method was to have the children abstain from the tests, appeal the one year ban, suggest Freedom of Choice, and after the children began the school year, it would be impossible to reassign them to their proper school. The belief was that blacks and whites would likely remain in their same schools. Table 7.3 shows how many students would be transferred after testing. In Holly Springs, 175 blacks were to be transferred to white schools, and 59 whites were to attend white schools. In the city schools, blacks comprised almost 70 percent of the population at the elementary level, and about 60 percent at the secondary level. In fact, more black students dropped out of school than there were whites in school.

The testing plan was to be continued at the end of April 1970, as grades 5 through 8 were to be tested in May 1970 and assigned in September 1970 along with grades 1 through 4. Then, in May 1971 all grades would be tested and assigned in September 1971. Facing the possibilities of desegregating through testing, and with the pending desegregation cases still in the courts, the Board of Trustees of Holly Springs and Marshall County Schools decided to conduct surveys of opinions of school patrons, voters, and taxpayers in order to determine the feelings of the district toward desegregation.

Table 7.3 Students Who Would Be Transferred in Holly Springs, by Race, the *South Reporter*

Grade	Whites transferred to Black Schools	Blacks transferred to White Schools
1	36	40
2	40	35
3	32	37
4	30	32
Total	138	140

In the wake of judicial rulings, the U.S. Courts had also allowed alternative schemes for integration besides the testing of Judge Keady, and Marshall County used these to delay integration too. The U.S. Courts had developed four plans for integrating schools; pairing, zoning, testing, and consolidation. The school board believed that by using the opinions of the surveys it could convince the U.S. Courts to delay desegregation. The failure in the U.S. Courts and at the state level left the school board grasping at anything to help against desegregation. The parent survey sent out by schools asked what court option should be used to desegregate the schools. The first plan was pairing, where all children in grades 1 through 3 attended one school together, and those in grades 4 through 6 attended another school together in a separate building. Pairing was not very popular with white parents, but blacks saw it as the closest thing to full desegregation. The second plan was less popular. Zoning was the use of designated areas known as zones, which were racially balanced with both races in each zone. Blacks saw it as a great plan for one reason, that in changing zones, it would serve to even out voting zones in the districts of Holly Springs. The third plan which was the one assigned to the county and city, testing, was based on achievement tests, whereby the highest scores attended one school, and the lower scores another. This plan was not liked by the white community, and abhorred by blacks. Blacks concurred reluctantly since it provided the only option at the time to desegregate the schools. The final plan, consolidation of grades, whereby one school became central, and all other schools were closed, was the closest system to total desegregation, and favored by a small minority of whites. The plan would close the black schools, and move all children to the Holly High-Sallie Cochran Complex. According to the Anthony ruling in 1968, a school system must establish one system by order of the court in order to have a public school system during the 1970–1971 school year. The court had accepted these four plans as viable to replace Freedom of Choice.

The results of the parent survey were announced in the November 20 *South Reporter*. Whites hoped results of the survey might deter blacks in Holly Springs. Also, white resistance could be reenergized behind the new struggle against the U.S. Courts. The white leadership feared their constituency was giving up. The results surprised no one. Whites overwhelmingly chose Freedom of Choice, which was not an option on the survey. For blacks, zoning and pairing led the lists as the most popular choices, three times more popular than testing and consolidation. Table 7.4 shows the breakdown of the survey results for Holly Springs.

As the year was winding down, Judge Hugo Black handed down a decision that changed the face of schooling in Holly Springs. This decision forced total desegregation without any room for appeals. The decision came from the U.S. Supreme Court and represented the final word on desegregation. On December 4, 1969, the court ordered the second phase for school desegregation to begin (US 419 F.2d 1211, 1970). Marshall County and Holly Springs were ordered to establish a unitary school system by September 1970. Faculties, staff, transportation, services athletics, and other extracurricular activities had to be merged by February 1, 1970. According to the U.S. Supreme Court, schools had to have the same racial percentage in schools as children who lived in the district. This meant that for the city and the county, 70 percent black and 30 percent white. Judge Black also handed down a second harsher penalty for the desegregation of the schools by revoking the use of testing, giving each school district until January 6, 1970, to file a plan with the U.S. Circuit Court that complied with the *Singleton v. Jackson Municipal Separate School District* decision.

Table 7.4 Survey of Parents Choice for Desegregation, Holly Springs, the *South Reporter*

Plan	Percentage for 1st choice	White Total	Black Total	Other	Total
Freedom of choice	34	194	0	8	202
Pairing	21	18	91	17	126
Zoning	18	12	88	8	108
Consolidation	13	44	35	1	80
Testing	7	23	21	0	44

Following his decision, Judge Black immediately announced a second decision in order to avoid the stalling tactics that followed other rulings. He announced that by February 1, 16 school desegregation cases would be decided. These districts had to submit plans and request help from the U.S. Office of Education. Following orders from Black, on December 4, 1969, Judge Keady set January 15, 1970, as the hearing date where the plan had to be presented to HEW with the understanding that in schools "No race or color shall be excluded." On February 1, 1970, all teachers, principals, and staff were reassigned "so as to not constitute any racial induction of school for white or black" (US 419 F.2d 1211, 1970). The ratio of black to white teachers was 64 to 36 percent. Table 7.5 shows the reassignment of teachers by schools for the city of Holly Springs and Marshall County.

Table 7.5 Teachers Transferred after Desegregation in County and City Schools, the *South Reporter*

School	White Teachers	Black Teachers	Total
Sallie Cochran	6	10	16
Frazier	12	28	40
Holly High	7	12	19
Sims	12	22	34
Holly Springs Total	**37**	**72**	**109**
Henry High	20	37	57
Byhalia	8	14	22
Sand Flat	13	24	37
Mary Reed	3	5	8
Slayden	6	10	16
Potts Camp	8	12	20
Galena	6	15	21
Marshall Co. Total	**64**	**117**	**181**

Two weeks later, following the Fifth Circuit Court's lead, the U.S. Supreme Court set February 1, 1970, as the deadline for total desegregation. The U.S. Courts instructed Marshall County and Holly Springs to take steps for complete school desegregation by the deadline. The U.S. Supreme Court would make the final decision on desegregation, thereby bypassing the district, in case schools petitioned about the impossibility of compliance in the allotted time. Schools had to file a plan with the Fifth Circuit Court on January 6, 1970, and respond to Judge Black about the decision by January 2, 1970. On January 5, 1970, Holly Springs and Marshall County school districts filed desegregation plans with the court and HEW. The plans divided the children among the schools. Table 7.6 shows the exact breakdown of the desegregation plan. The district chose Joseph Ford, who had been ostracized earlier after being accused of writing letters against the firing of teachers in 1960 to desegregate Holly High, a the symbol of white Holly Springs.

Table 7.6 Proposed Student Breakdown for Holly Springs Schools, the
    South Reporter

Grades	School	White	Black	Total
1–3	Sallie Cochran	150	518	668
4–6	Frazier	150	533	683
7–9	Sims	138	495	633
10–12	Holly High	135	279	414
Total		573	1825	2398

As Table 7.6 demonstrates, the white population remained steady throughout the school life of the child (grades 1–12). For example, there are only fifteen less students between the first and twelfth grades. For blacks the difference is almost half between the first and twelfth grades. Table 7.7 shows the breakdown of desegregation at the county level. The county was much different than the city. Because of its size and the sparse population, the desegregation of the county was much more difficult. It was, however, more successful. The private schools were in the city, not in the county. The county schools were also smaller than the city schools.

Table 7.7 Proposed Student Breakdown for Marshall County Schools, the
South Reporter

School	Grades	White	Black	Total
Byhalia	9–12	120	548	668
Henry	1–8	416	1114	1530
Sand Flat	1–6, 10–12	255	770	1025
Slayden	7–9	85	217	302
Galena	1–8	64	425	489
Mary Reed	1–4	163	118	281
Potts Camp	5–12	236	184	420
Total		1339	3312	4651

The white resistance finally ran out of steam as the U.S. Courts ruled in favor of total desegregation in the county. The school districts had to abide or lose control of their schools. Teachers in grades 1 through 6 would be assigned children through a lottery. In grades 7 through 12, students would choose the teachers for each subject as had been done before. The principal of Holly Springs High School, grades 10 through 12, was Joseph Ford, because he had the highest credentials. The Intermediate School, grades 4 through 9, was to be headed by Donald Randolph, the former Holly High principal; and Alice Bell, who was the principal at Sallie Cochran, headed the Primary School, grades 1 through 4. All students stayed with the same teachers they had. Schools were to close on January 23 to move furniture and reopen on February 2 in Marshall County and Holly Springs, as desegregated schools for the first time ever.

CHAPTER EIGHT

Freedom of Choice,
a New Perspective: Narrative of Our Senior Year, 1966

Introduction

Beneath the formal language of the U.S. Courts' rulings, plans of desegregation, appeals and defendants' protests, real men and women—real boys and girls—were living, working, and making their way in the chaotic collapse of southern apartheid. This chapter explores their circumstances through the voices of two individuals who participated in Freedom of Choice. Freedom of Choice afforded blacks the opportunity for partial integration. It chiefly applied to black students. Not a single white student from Holly Springs attended the black schools. The relative peace that was kept around the school was eerily quiet compared to the rest of the state where children were chased down and beaten by mobs.

Freedom of Choice?

The world of Freedom of Choice was very different for all the participants involved. Black students, Al Beck and Ruth Harper Greer, during their senior year at Holly Springs High School in 1966 chose to attend the white school over their own W.T. Sims High School. The experience that year at the high school served both Al Beck and Ruth Harper Greer, as well as their three other black classmates, as a sample of what society had in store for them outside of the South. If they could succeed in schools, which according to Harper Greer, was the harshest of all environments, they could succeed anywhere. Also, from their experiences they took with them a sense of repaying their community, choosing to return and, in turn, helping rekindle a sense of community and collective for blacks in Holly Springs thirty years later. Constance Curry (1995) described a similar feeling about her experiences in the white school during Freedom of Choice. As Ruth Harper Greer, who today is the head nurse at the County Hospital, recalls,

I was in the first integrated class, and it was kind of weird how I ended up going to Holly High .... the way I ended up going there was that my dad would not let me get on the buses during the Freedom Rides . . . cause we had a lot of what we call safe housing and those were housing where people from like Michigan, Michigan State, Indiana, Chicago, all of these college students would come down

and they would live in these houses . . . people would just let them stay, they
would just by their own food and everything . . . and those would be the places
where they would have the meetings and get people ready to go to Birmingham
or where ever . . . but my dad was like Im sorry you cannot go . . . so in sixty-six,
the summer you could go to whatever school you wanted to . . . but for Sims it
would take you twenty minutes to walk up to . . . you know they haven't done
anything . . . I'll give them a year, I'll give them a year of my life . . . if I had
known it would have been that much hell I would never have gone. . . .

Al Beck remembered other reasons for attending Holly High. He
already participated in the movement and wanted to attend Holly High
School for personal improvement. Similar to Ruth Harper Greer, he also
wanted to leave Holly Springs, a special quality of adventure for anyone
who was able to participate in the hostile world of Freedom of Choice.
Ruth Harper Greer explained that blacks lived next to a school they could
not attend, which insulted and inspired some blacks. Curry (1995)
described the choice in terms of purely individual strength. The two
students approached both of their parents with the suggestion to attend the
white school. It was an individual act, not supported by either blacks or
whites, seen as usurping segregation and the support system established to
combat it. If the system that was supposed to protect blacks segregated
them, why would any individual willingly accept the consequences of
displacing both the white and black status quo? As Al Beck recalled,

Why I chose to go to Holly High. . . . Well, I guess for most of my life living in
Holly Springs, you look at the outside world, which is a lot larger of course . . .
and you see the cities New York, Chicago, L.A. and the rest of the world . . . Paris
. . . and I always wondered how I would compare to students who graduated from
those places . . . never thinking I would remain in Holly Springs after I grew up
. . . I had to prepare myself to compete when I go somewhere else . . . so I was
looking for an opportunity to make myself better able to compete . . . and my
parents always thought the same way . . . they encouraged reading always kept a
lot of books around . . . and always tried to help me to see further than the city
limits . . . so to speak. . . .

As he regarded his future, he said, he recognized the differences of the
white school: "they had better books, better equipment . . . laboratories,
you know . . . everything that would promote better education . . . so this
was an excellent opportunity . . . and there were several students who were
asked to go . . . I'm told, I don't know for sure . . . but no one asked me to

go or mentioned it to me . . . 'you should go to Holly High' . . . and it was just something . . . it was opened . . . it was publicly announced that it was open and my thought was 'I gotta do this' . . . you know 'you gotta do this." Beneath the personal and family attention, however, Beck also couched his decision in terms of racial uplift and community. "I had worked in the Civil Rights Movement, he recalled, I had done some things around that would hopefully help to promote integration and hopefully just a better life for the black community . . . and so it weighed heavy on my mind when the opportunity came about. . . ." And the results? "I did learn a lot that year . . . I had a good year, academically, he insisted, but added, it was a hell of a year socially. . . ."

Beck's work in civil rights gave him the inner strength and conviction to "stick it out" for the school year. He needed all such resources and nerves. It was, indeed, ". . . a hell of a year socially." He recalled one incident in particular:

> I came to my locker at midday and there was this big Master-lock pad-lock on my locker and so they had to come over and cut it off.... one of the coaches had to come over with a hack-saw and cut it off . . . well, actually what they ended up doing was they didn't cut the lock, they ended up cutting the locker . . . so as a consequence, I could never lock my locker again . . . so, you know what I'm saying . . . the rest of the year . . . there were several die-hard students that I guess they took it on their own to make sure that I understood that I wasn't wanted there.

He recalled other events in this hellish season. "Did you ever play football," he asked?

> You know the drill where they'll have a line, two lines and you get the ball, and they bump you and trip . . . try to . . . I guess that's called a fumble exercise . . . contact exercise . . . that's kind of what it was like going through the hallway . . . to virtually every class . . . you know, somebody was bumping you on a regular basis . . . sometimes you could see them coming sometimes you could not . . . some of them you knew that it was coming from cause they did it every day . . . so you know . . . and I played football before at Sims, so I had no problem using the forearm and you know . . . I held my own with that I never left there with any bruises that I could recall. . . .

If daily life at Holly High was like a football scrimmage for Al Beck, actual football–or its absence–entered his memories too.

It was interesting, very interesting . . . obviously that was quite a bit of
solitude, didn't really have the regular exchange between the other students, I
mean I was the only black there . . . so not a whole lot of conversation, a lot of
time to think and listen and do whatever you were going to do . . . and just figure
out what kind of games were going on next.

Teachers, students . . . the whole nine yards . . . I remember when I first got to ask
if I could play football . . . because I had transferred from one school in the same
district to another school . . . they brought up some rule . . . and I cannot imagine
that the rule was on the books . . . it was just verbally stated to me . . . and I cannot
imagine that they would have looked ahead to even develop that type of rule
unless it was just a state rule . . . because, you know, you only had one white
school and two black schools and St. Mary's parochial school . . . and the city
school, and we exchanged students all the time . . . if they played here last year
they'd come to the next school, you know, without missing a beat . . . and no one
had ever questioned that, and I can not imagine that they had that rule in the
public schools because they never anticipated integration. . . .

It was a lonely year too. "Actually, there was one guy that befriended
me and he would come over in class and talk to me which was almost
amazing . . . and that lasted for about two or three weeks . . . . and then he
called me, he used to call me after class and we would talk on the phone."
It did not last long. After a little while, Beck remembered, "he came to me
and told me that his sister was being heckled quite a bit, and he felt that it
was because of his display towards me . . . so . . . he fell by the wayside .
. . he wasn't afraid for himself but he was afraid for his sister, blah, blah,
blah . . . so we didn't have very much contact after that . . . but he was the
only one . . . the only student that ever even spoke to me . . . the only white
student." Like Al, Ruth also experienced the loneliness of school. "I had
some of my classes with Modina, but I didn't have any classes with Al . .
. it kind of depended on which classes we had . . . . and we did have lunch
at the same time . . . . so it was kind of, usually one or two of us would be
in the same lunch at the same time." Ruth's experiences parallel those of
Al in dealing with companionship.

There was some people who would write mail and would use derogatory terms
. . . and those were kind of trashy people, I mean they were the kind of people I
don't think anybody would want their kids to be with . . . they were just trashy.
. . . But there was one girl in my class named Puddin' and she had inherited all
of this money from her grandparents or somebody . . . and she had her own car,
a maid, a cook, a really, really rich girl, the owner, that she was like hey, if you

want to talk to somebody, Ill talk to you, and I was like, OK, she wanted to exchange pictures and phone numbers, but that was the only person that I knew, other than Modina or Janice or them. . . .

Among the problems encountered by the black students attending Holly High were their experiences within their community. When they returned to their homes, many of their peers wondered why they wanted to be with the whites.

Yeah, they called us deserters, you know . . . it was, my thought was that   . . . and I didn't look at myself as a hero or anything, but I did look at myself as 'Yeah, you're stepping out there,' go ahead on . . . someday we'll . . . but it was like 'they left us, they are not part of us any more'. . . I really didn't understand that, and it was really disheartening . . . I really didn't understand that, and I still don't to this day . . . I remember after graduating from college, coming back to a class reunion, and I wasn't invited . . . I just heard about it, as a matter of fact I just happened to be home and they were having it . . . and I walked to the door and they were like, well you didn't graduate with us you have to pay a visitor's fee . . . I didn't have no problem with the money but the attitude was like, 'Whoa, hey what's going on here?' and since that time its changed with the class reunions, but the first couple . . . I was almost like . . . and even the conversations, I mean it wasn't just that person at the door . . . there were quasi-negative comments . . . a little bit of tact here and there . . . sometimes very direct though . . . not much tact at all. . . .

The big surprise that awaited the Freedom of Choicers was teachers' acceptance. Teachers helped ease the choice to attend the white school, especially in the academic arena, where to their surprise the students received better grades than they expected. There was enforcement of new rules for transfer students enacted by the state legislature, locker searches, bag searches, and administrative impediments for the transfer of students. Even though they did retaliate against black students by firing their parents or attacking the students, whites slowly began raising money to establish it as a white alternative to the public schools. Ruth Harper Greer recalls her experience with her teachers and their ability to make her feel welcomed, which for her did not correspond to the rest of the school experience,

the teachers were really good, they tried to make me feel as welcome as they could . . . you know . . . my teacher was Mrs. [Chesley Thorne] Smith . . . and she said 'if you have any problems do not hesitate to call me at home, this is my home number, this is my home room'. . . she really did, and I felt that I could have talked to her about anything, but when I did the year book, they put all of our pictures on the back page . . . so that you could just take that page off . . . and you could have your year book without blacks. . . . Well, that's us . . . in the year book, we were the four people on the back page of the senior . . . you could rip that one page out and then you wouldn't have them in your book. . . .

Al Beck echoed Ruth Harper Greer's praise of teachers' dedication,

. . . I liked to think that I had pretty good intuition at that age in spite of being very young . . . and I can recall being in various classes and feeling, you know, that this person is doing just the minimal of what they can for me . . . however, there were some teachers and I don't want to high-light that because there were more teachers that were more apparently dedicated teachers. . . .

I got the feeling, and my experience with learning with them and going to class with them . . . the whole class and learning experience was they wanted you to learn period they didn't care what the class was made up of . . . once you walked in and you close the door and you were at your seat they were about teaching students . . . there were several teachers that I felt that way about . . . Mrs. [Faunta] O'Dell was one . . . I never felt that she did anything to hinder me at all.

He recalled another,

Mrs. [Chesley Thorne] Smith, . . . I remember her, she was just a very dedicated teacher . . . I took geometry from her . . . made an A . . . quite frankly I knew I was doing A work . . . but I didn't think I would received the grade...pleased, not really surprised I guess at the end of the year, but I was very pleased that she did give me the grade. . . . based on just scores through out the year and performance in class . . . and on, and on, and on . . . I felt that she was a good lady and she never showed me any prejudice that I could recognize at the time, you know, she was very helpful. . . .

Although he felt that teachers were there to help him, Beck held reservations about others. He recalls,

the guy that I really thought belonged to the Ku Klux Klan . . . and maybe that's . . . just by his actions because I felt that he was very deceptive, you know, could not be trusted, devil incarnate sort of person . . . was the principal Joe Williams [left soon for a school in the Delta], and maybe he just thought he was trying to do a good job with a new and rough situation, but at the same time I felt that he was not going to let . . . I just always felt that he was trying to keep a tight reign on us. . . .

One experience that really affected Al Beck was his connection to the librarian through an unspoken exchange during study hall. Of the devoted and dedicated instructors Al Beck recalled one who symbolized what amounted to intellectual virtue for him.

> The lady who really, I guess when I first arrived, she didn't . . . how can I put this . . . she was . . . to give me . . . she was a librarian, Ill tell you who she was . . . I think her name was Colthart . . . C-o-l-t-h-a-r-p . . . she was the librarian, I don't know how she pronounced it though . . . I was in study hall one day . . . . and she, the first day I was there, she brought me a book and she said 'I think you may be interested in this' . . . and it was a book about the first black general in the modern military, Benjamin O. Davis . . . . and it was his biography, or maybe it was his autobiography . . . and I read that of course he told about all of the hard times he faced going through the academy . . . and the military . . . and I guess that really, it helped . . . it definitely helped . . . and what I got from that was that she was saying 'Just hang in there.'

In Holly Springs, whites perceived that race and class were one in the same when it came to blacks. Ruth Harper Greer recalls her experiences; she deserted her fellow blacks and, therefore, was treated to a cold reception from them. The actions were visible for Ruth during the school day. Ruth Harper Greer recalled she did not attend civil rights marches or demonstrate, she integrated Holly High because, "that's what I did ... for the movement . . . . not . . . . going to marches or other places . . . . but that's how I ended up going to Holly High." Ruth, like Al, found no companionship at school. "In my class, the students did not talk to me . . . you know I was just like an object . . . I would see them and the teachers would let them look through my purse." She described herself as "totally isolated," not only at Holly High but among her black friends too, "but then my friend at the other school, my black friends . . . they would tell me that they didn't know what was wrong with me . . . so here I am, you know . . . anytime that we were out of school at Holly High I'd go back over to my other school, and they were like 'why are you down here' . . . leave . . . so it was a real hard. . . . "

The experience in the schools allowed Ruth Harper Greer and Al Beck a new understanding of their lives. They lived out a difficult experience and today feel they owe it to their community to help heal old wounds from the 1960s. They have both returned to Holly Springs, and plan on living their lives there. Along with the current mayor, Eddie Lee Smith, also a civil rights leader, they are attempting to build a new leadership base for their community. Reflecting on her experience, Ruth Harper Greer recounts her thoughts on Holly Springs, and why she returned,

> the one thing that is so sad about this community is that I went away for twenty-two years and then I came back, because my husband really wanted to coach football here . . . so he had the opportunity to do that, so that's why we ended up coming back . . . but what is so sad to me is that nothing has changed, and I have my theory, and my theory is that integration is something that you can't force . . . you can not force it, you cant mandate it, you cant make a law about it . . . but when you in your soul, not in your mind, in your soul, you believe it . . . because your mother has told you, your grandmother everybody that you know, you have lived this way . . . the only black people you have known, not seen, but known are people that work for you . . . they call you mistress since you were twelve years old . . . you cant look around and . . . that's you, that is who you are . . . most people, when you know better, you do better . . . for example I work with people here who welcome me into their homes they come into my home . . . now these are adults, now, they had to become adults to realize that . . . whenever grandmother held this person down . . . now whether that will ever happen, I don't know. . . .

Her connection to Holly Springs is one of place. In *Black Boy* (1998), Richard Wright felt the same attraction to his home in Roxie, Mississippi. This was even after the atrocities he witnessed against blacks. The attraction to place is extremely strong for many southerners, as Michael Kreyling (1998) illustrates in *Inventing Southern Literature*, "the myth and the history feed one another; together they make consciousness a process, and we are in it, body and mind" (p. 18). Whether this connection was real or not, it is tied into their identity as southern blacks and their experiences as Freedom of Choice participants. As Ruth explains the reason why there is a white academy in Holly Springs,

> why shouldn't you have your own school, if you can buy it, you can have your own school . . . you can dictate who will play sports, you can dictate who can be in clubs, you can dictate this because you are paying for it . . . why should you take a chance to get out of that one uterus . . . to go out into this cold world . . . you know babies would never be born if they didn't have to . . . in that uterus they are just enjoying, so nice and warm . . . and my theory is that if I can afford to not even deal with you so I'm not going to . . . and . . . a lot of their children go off to school and they even learn the hard way that people are the same . . . or they never learn they think and they go to a place, where everybody knows you . . . so they can keep you out of their uterus . . . and never have to change.

Along with her views on the school, Ruth believes that change can occur. As the head nurse at the county hospital she tells the nurses sometimes,

> it's the southern belle theory . . . I can get so passive aggressive but I can get what I want . . . you know I will never hurt your feelings but I can still get what I want. . . . So . . . my momma worked for your momma, and her momma worked for your grand mamma, and so on . . . I cannot hurt your feelings because I know your going to keep my children like your momma and on and on and on . . . so Im just going to be as nice as I can be . . . that's what Im going to do . . . you have to come over here anyway . . . you know why I can afford it, you know why . . . because I already made my money . . . your great grandparents money, I have my money . . . Holly Springs has all these millionaires.

> I really think that this is what they believe . . . this is what is in their soul . . . if something should happen to their child . . . or whatever . . . because you just believe it . . . , I need your money, I need you to use my bank . . . I need you to go to my clothing store, and to be perfectly honest with you, when you go to my bank I'm going to help you, because its different, but now if you are going to touch my child . . . well now, I just don't know . . . I honestly just don't know what it is . . . but Holly Springs . . . I lived in Memphis for twenty-two years and it was just so different . . . I don't know what it is . . . there sits there at his barber shop, and on his other side, and a liquor store. . . .

The old conflicts continue 35 years after when Ruth Greer meets people she attended school with. She is now the head nurse in the largest hospital in town. Her position at the hospital allows her to connect with persons who have left the public schools for the private schools. She believes it has become a question of quality over race. She also realizes that times can change. She is optimistic over the future, although the reality of Holly Springs today is the visible segregation in all aspects of life, and the mistrust of blacks and whites throughout the city. Along with her optimism for the future is her assessment of the current race relations. "It doesn't matter what I have to do, Im not going to let my children go to school with yours. . . . It doesn't matter, if I have to go to work, I'll go to work, if I have to get two jobs, I'll work two jobs . . . but its one thing that people fail to realize . . . it doesn't make you anything because they don't know you . . . how are you ever going to get to know me if you already know me as a piece of furniture, you already know me as a maid."

The telling experience of Freedom of Choice centered on the students' discovery or reinforcement of their skin color, and of their place in history, expressed in their internalization of the moment. They understood what it meant to be black in the South.

> See I did not know what I was . . . black doctors, teachers, nurses, you know everything . . . I just thought that you would grow up and you would be what you wanted to be . . . I didn't know that I was this poor little underprivileged black kid, that I was supposed to get pregnant when I was thirteen, and have all these illegitimate babies . . . I didn't know this, you know, I just thought . . . my dad worked . . . and my mom she baby sat, you know she wasn't much, but I didn't know that she couldn't be what she wanted to be . . . I didn't know that I wasn't supposed to do this . . . so when I got there they have some really big problems . . . and I kind of figured it out after a half year or so . . . and she don't live with . . . I could look at her and see how segregated they were among themselves . . . and rich one were here, and the other ones were here . . . to see how they would be . . . I said let me get the hell out of here and get on with my life . . . but it was like they have some really big problems . . . I always believed that I could do whatever I wanted to do, because its what I had been taught all my life . . . a lot of people don't have that advantage to feel.

Although his memories are different, Al Beck reinforced his beliefs in himself that would lead him to succeed. He felt that there was a bigger purpose to the Movement. At first, Al Beck saw Freedom of Choice as a personal adventure, but as he recalls his experiences, he saw it as his continuing work with the Civil Rights Movement.

> I was at the march in Washington. I was part of the advance team for the mule train . . . did voter registration throughout Marshall county, Sunflower county, around Greenwood . . . they're all down in that area . . . I mean I was all over the place . . . got a policeman down in Lowndes County in Alabama to put a crease in my head . . . with a billy-club that remains to this day . . . it seems like when the Alabama state troopers had to be six-two or better . . . they were all these really big guys . . . yeah, I was at Selma . . . I was back and forth to Atlanta and different places . . . I didn't think it was my little part, but it was because of all that I had done I felt that I would be a hypocrite if I didn't . . . and that didn't move me so much as that with my personal . . . I felt it would help me to be there, you know . . . I went along with the movement to go to Holly High that year . . . it would help myself . . . it would help the community . . . it was just the thing to do.
>
> That's when you really discover who you are as a person . . . in the world . . . that's when you get in fights to discover whether you're going to make it . . . you

know, that's when you find your resolve so to speak . . . and I guess I did, its just
a little different path. . . .

While their decision to attend Holly High estranged them from their
friends at Sims, the Freedom of Choice students found little support among
local civil rights workers in Holly Springs. "The civil rights workers were
cheerleaders," remembers Al, "but I was really disappointed by the local
people that I had really grown to have a tremendous amount of respect for
. . . it was almost like they were afraid to acknowledge me, especially in
public . . . I got the feeling that . . . how could I say this . . . had I been
standing in the middle of a square somewhere and I called one of their
names out loud, that they might have ignored me . . . that kind of thing
. . . that was an eye-opener as to human nature."

In her autobiography, Constance Curry (1995) feared that her parents
might suffer for her decision to integrate. The anxiety never entered Al
Beck's mind. His parents supported his decision, and, as he recalls, his
mother did not lose her job.

> Yeah she worked at the school . . . Well, like I say, you know in our
> conversation in Holly Springs, we evolved out of the civil rights movement . . .
> and I guess that would have been just of out of character for Holly Springs to be
> that forward . . . that was the reason why I felt terribly comfortable . . . because we
> over the years had various black prisoners that hung themselves . . . and I'm
> generalizing . . . and we never want anybody to think this is a generalization that
> many black people that kill themselves . . . they might for the last ten or fifteen
> years . . . you just don't hear of . . . you know, we just don't become that distraught
> . . . "Life is just too rough, I gotta end it right here" you know . . . it just does not
> happen . . . so here is a streak that likes the liquor, likes to hang out, you know
> . . . throw a fist or two, and just like to be out and about . . . but yet he gets
> arrested and he says "Lord I just cant take it I'm going to hang myself" . . . you
> know he gets arrested for being drunk and disorderly and he comes up hung and
> he must have hung himself . . . but it just doesn't happen, give me a break, you
> know . . . and that happened two or three times . . . but we didn't have a lot of . .
> . you know you didn't find that many people in the river . . . you know . . . hung
> in trees . . . not over the last fifty or sixty years . . . so in a way I wasn't really that
> concerned about that, because it hadn't really manifested itself that way . . .
> previously, you know.

Returning to Holly Springs thirty-five years after they left, Al and Ruth
reflected on what could be different, and show how their experiences led
to similar views on what Holly Springs and blacks must do in order to

improve their situation. In their decision to return to their hometown, like new mayor and former civil rights organizer Eddie Lee Smith, they see a second phase in the leadership of the black community. For Ruth Harper Greer, desegregation led to the birth of Marshall Academy and the white flight from the public schools, as well as the abandonment of the key social institution for the advancement of the entire community, which cannot occur when one race attends the public schools and the other the private schools.

Al also recalled how other institutions were destroyed rather than integrated, ". . . burned the theater . . . so they wouldn't have to integrate it . . . but you know, Mississippi has always been like that . . . they built a swimming pool, when we were trying to integrate the swimming pool and they built one . . . . 'Here you got your own swimming pool' . . . and you know we had a gym . . . and you know . . . your comments exactly, this is a very polite town . . . so 'give them a little something to appease them,' 'give them a little something,' that just went on forever . . . and it still goes on till this day."

Ruth Harper Greer's recollections remind her that one reason why the town is still segregated is that there is a fear to change from blacks as much as from whites. After "Marshall Academy . . . and they made sure of it . . . anybody wants to come here . . . and its like you said its legal, but I think that we just accept it . . . and Im just not going to deal with it . . . and I've been very disappointed in the black population you know your selves why are you crying on yourself . . . you know there are other jobs you can do . . . there are other things we can do . . . but I'm talking about why don't we out our money together and do something . . . there's a fear of change."

Change for Ruth Harper Greer can only occur after the public schools become public again.

> I really think the bigger problem though is the school system. Yes, number one, until we get a superintendent in there who can increase scores . . . I don't care who he is . . . and that's life . . . you want to know when you go to a school . . . am I going to be able to read when I get out . . . you don't care about color . . . but you care about . . . my teacher but we said break away from family pride . . . we need this to survive.

> Well, I can tell you this, the people I went to high school with . . . and I see them now . . . they are like willing to just start the whole system over . . . and they knew me, because I sat there in their class for a whole year . . . you know, its OK for you

to talk to me anymore if we could just let that trickle down . . . why don't we just
let in a good superintendent, a good principal . . . I'm not trying to say that they
are bad, but couldn't we do better and then wouldn't our children learn . . . I went
to school last year . . . take the money that we have put into the public school
system and invest it . . . we'd have one of the best in the country.

If they had the number one public school system then they would have to ensure
the safety of their children . . . there comes a time . . . number two, the protests
. . . if they honestly do that and go on marching . . . then I think they can do it ...
but you gotta get up now, you gotta get up . . . because its almost like saying
something that they all thought they need . . . I don't know.

In Ruth's mind, "when [she] was in the public school system, it was
much worse than it is now . . . much worse . . . we had much worse teachers
. . . we had . . . second hand, third hand books . . . when we got a new book
. . . a cover on a cover . . . a new book . . . I thought I'm the first person to
use this book . . . gotta wash our hands after doing homework . . . because
Im telling you, we got hand me downs . . . so, we . . . it was the pits . . . but
I went home and read."

Al Beck eloquently compared his experience in Marshall county to the
Delta. He believed that there was the opportunity to turn Holly Springs
into something great, a Mecca for blacks, but they missed their chance,
which in the end led to the current situation.

I remember, I used to go out when COFO, as they call it . . . counsel's over
on West Avenue and we'd go out in the county and we'd bring people into town
and register them to vote and on, and on, and on . . . and the roles were right there
so you could kind of peek over and see . . . and its amazing to me to see the
number of people you would have expected to see on the rolls, weren't on the rolls
. . . and you knew they could read, write . . . you know, they could handle it . . .
but the majority of the people, and don't get me wrong there were a lot of people
that did . . . and leaders, some that did, but there were a lot that didn't . . . but I
guess that's in every group . . . some come on earlier and some come on later
. . . and a lot of people had a lot of good reasons for it . . . a lot of peoples had
their livelihood depended on it . . . in the school system, or whatever . . . or some
type of local economic resource that their jobs or livelihood could have been
affected by it.

Well I think that the concept made sense in that the Delta was always seen as the
big troubled area so you needed to put your biggest effort there, and then you look
at a place like Holly Springs and, well, it was obviously a good stop off, because
at the time you had two black colleges, probably . . . and I don't know what you'd

do about Holly Springs because Holly Springs as far as Mississippi was
concerned, a place of reckoning, you know . . . it was known, you just drive
around and you see the generals stayed here . . . Lee stayed here and Grant stayed
here . . . the antebellum homes . . . they had a white college here years ago. . . .

The perception was that few blacks would attempt to integrate the
school. The white leadership believed that Freedom of Choice would soon
be over (Curry, 1995; Wieder, 1997; Wolters, 1984). The local white
leadership also understood the fear that blacks had about losing their jobs,
or loans, or access to any other private and public institution under white
control. In Holly Springs, the fear was more myth than reality, as the white
community did not act with the violence or the economic hegemony that
occurred in Delta towns (Bartley, 1995; Cobb, 1992). Many of the blacks
were economically independent from whites, especially the middle class,
which was employed at places like Rust and MI College, and the black
dollar was more important to the local economy than whites espoused.

Social class played a role in Freedom of Choice in Holly Springs.
Many of the children attending the high school were middle class or above
by Mississippi standards. As Raymond Wolters (1984) has shown in cases
of desegregation, and Willie Morris (1971) described in his hometown of
Yazoo City during desegregation in 1970, events were surprisingly
peaceful. As he illustrates, the attitude of the upper social class was crucial
in the reaction to desegregation, leading to peaceful desegregation because
its leadership urged everyone to stay in the public schools. The
hierarchical nature of Holly Springs, and its service class-based power
structure (bankers, landholders, store owners) minimized violence. Lower-
class whites figured significant in antiblack violence elsewhere, but that did
not occur in Holly Springs (Carson, 1981). Second, the proximity and
mutual reliance of the black and white communities also kept the relations
amicable if tense. Third, as was demonstrated by Elizabeth Jacoway and
David Colburn (1982), southern businessmen were reluctant to use violence
in their towns in the 1960s. They tended to be more moderate in terms of
change (Jacoway and Colburn, p. 295). Their experiences were mostly
forgotten by both blacks and whites, and as they left high school after
graduation, no one told their story. Their individual attempt benefitted
their own lives after graduation, but these individual efforts soon gave way
to the federal government's use of the U.S. Courts to force full

desegregation through decree. This was at the expense of the local leadership, which was not financially or politically equipped like whites in other cities to implement the legal actions of the government.

CHAPTER NINE

February 1, 1970:
The Aftermath of Legal Desegregation, 1970–1974

Introduction

The entire South experienced the social and education turmoil that affected Holly Springs between the Brown case and the seventies. Marshall County's experiences, however, after desegregation contrasted with that of other towns or counties in the South and even in Mississippi. This chapter examines Mississippi, then the South, and finally Holly Springs and Marshall County to understand the connections between national and local trends in desegregation. The desegregation of schools was the last major challenge to the southern order by the federal government. It rivaled the fight to invalidate the poll tax by the U.S. Supreme Court in August 1966. This is a watershed in federal and state government relationships as the federal government established itself as the driving force behind schooling.

Raymond Wolters (1984) attempted a similar study by discussing five crucial desegregation cases that occurred in the U.S. Mark Whitman (1998) also attempts to describe desegregation of schools by tracing the development of the implementation of Brown II (1955) and its consequences in the 1990s. The importance of the legal battle for desegregation is muddled in the political movement to create equity through education (Wolters, 1984). The section on the desegregation of Holly Springs examines the legal implications from the point of view of those involved in desegregating the schools, and their mistrust of public schools after desegregation.

School Desegregation: January 1970

On the evening of January 3, 1970, Governor John Bell Williams addressed the issue of desegregation in a speech broadcast throughout Mississippi. He told his listeners that there was no statewide solution to the school crisis. Instead, he argued for private and public school coexistence in his speech. Admitting that the state of Mississippi lost the fight over school Freedom of Choice, Governor Williams instructed Mississippians to "decide for themselves what type of school their child will attend. . . . In facing the immediate ordeal, I am compelled to repeat . . . there is no panacea for a statewide solution prior to the opening of our schools for the next semester." At that time thirty state school districts awaited Health, Education, and Welfare (HEW) plans for public school integration "based on racial percentages instead of the state's freedom of choice method" (*Jackson Clarion Ledger*, January 4, 1970).

The governor asked for cooperation between the private and public schools. The problem lay in the white academies' philosophy to keep segregation alive. They espoused that no one should be out of schools, and that if the population chose to attend private school, the state should help. The governor did nothing more to secure desegregation. The suggestion that blacks help support white academies was the last gasp at fighting the federal government by the white resistance. The governor appealed for some brotherhood against the federal government:

> For instance, it might be well for our school administrators, in communities where needs are great and the facilities limited, to make arrangements with legitimate private school administrators for the use of their physical facilities at times and hours when they are not required for public school purposes.
>
> The same spirit of cooperation . . . should exist between our churches and private schools, even as it exists now between our churches and the public schools.
>
> I am strongly of the opinion that we must preserve our public school system as an absolute necessity for the good of all . . . though I shall ask the Legislature to seek ways and means of rendering assistance toward this end (money for tuition).
>
> . . . On the other hand, a strong private school system may very well supplement and add strength to our public schools.
>
> The task at hand is monumental. It brings into immediate focus the problems confronting 148 public school districts, 795 school board members, 970 attendance centers, 40,000 public school teachers and staff personnel, 600,000 enrolled students, and an indeterminate number of parents and guardians.

Two days after the governor's speech, the school mix decree went into effect for thirty state districts. That Monday, Adams County churches voted on a school where 2,400 of the white students in the county were seeking entry. In Natchez, Adams County, Mississippi, sixteen Baptist congregations on Sunday voted on a resolution "supporting the establishment of a private, all-white school for the city and county, after receiving more than 2,400 applications for enrollment" (*Jackson Clarion Ledger*). That number represented roughly one-half of the white students remaining in the Natchez-Adams public school system. Trinity, an Episcopal School, had been in operation for some time at the elementary level. Starting that Sunday, however, registrations were being taken for proposed high school classes. A second school, Adams County Private School, which opened in the fall with an enrollment of 400, also anticipated an influx of new students with the advent of the new term and court-ordered integration of public school facilities.

In Jackson, the change was less drastic. Jackson, Mississippi, was the only major urban area in Mississippi. For the first three months of the school term, September through December, a total of 10,171 students were enrolled in public schools. According to the *Jackson Clarion Ledger*, of these 5,345 were in all-black schools, while another 4,826, of whom 4,286 were white, were enrolled in integrated schools. These figures indicated a "Negro attendance in integrated schools totaling 500." In Jackson, U.S. Marshals were on hand to prevent trouble. A force of fifty Marshals moved in during the weekend, "not because of any overt threat of violence but to prevent any recurrence of past troubles" (*Jackson Clarion Ledger*, January 7, 1970). The state had come to grips somewhat with the decision as some parents and church groups in Jackson "have advised their members to accept the desegregation order, which is a result of the US Supreme Court ruling October 29 that the schools must be desegregated now" (*Jackson Clarion Ledger*, January 7, 1970). Governor John Bell Williams followed his speech with a plea on the radio. He stated that "preservation of public school is essential. . . . Let us remember that the public schools, after all, are still public property and wilful damage or destruction of these properties is senseless" (*Jackson Clarion Ledger*, January 4, 1970).

Not all was peaceful. In Canton, a city of 8,000, 23 miles north of Jackson, one private school was established in an empty factory building owned by mayor-elect Hermit Jones, who gave "up his plant rather than comply with federal fair employment hiring requirements." Private schools had applications from 1,200 of the 1,400 white pupils in Canton. In Hattiesburg, the state's fourth largest city, four new private schools opened the first week of January 1970. In Yazoo City, 20 miles west from Canton, and the home of Willie Morris, State Senator Herman Decell led a drive to get white parents to pledge to keep their children in desegregated schools.

About 200 persons signed the pledge. At the same time, one of the private school pupil loan assistance programs passed by the 1969 legislature was being fought and held up in federal court until February 1, 1970.

In Tchula, State Representative Robert Clark, the only black member of the State Legislature, criticized Governor Williams' January 3 address. Clark told the *Clarion Ledger* that "the governor called for two school systems, and we don't even have one good school system in the state now" (January 5, 1970). The state began to rally its forces by pointing to evidence that segregation was practiced everywhere in the nation, and that the state and the South were being punished because of their past. One such case used as an example was the Pasadena School District Mix Suit, which went before the court on January 6. It was the first case on the West Coast. The Justice Department's statement made by the attorneys gave little hint as to why they had gone into Pasadena; stating that the "only interest is to see that all the kids get the best education they can." Dr. Joseph Engholm, told the paper that "I really believe that Pasadena . . . would make a fine landmark case for the government" (*Jackson Clarion Ledger*, January 7, 1970).

During the first week of desegregation, schools seemed fairly calm under the watchful eye of HEW. Most of the counties had only begun registering students but a few began classes under the sweeping U.S. Supreme Court order directed at thirty of the state's 149 districts. At Columbia, following the new routine that would become practice in the state, the previous all-white and all-Negro high schools were merged and the student body presidents spoke to the combined student bodies. In Marion County, the merged student body of 600 included about 200 black students. In Canton, the Canton Foundation opened one school with 141 students in grades 1 through 8, with plans to open another school with grades 1 through 12 on January 19 in a former tent factory owned by the mayor-elect. Responding to reports that classes within the school would remain segregated, Superintendent Fran Dunbaugh said, "I'm not supposing anybody has not complied" (*Jackson Clarion Ledger*, January 5, 1970).

In Hinds County, 15 of 170 Hinds County teachers reassigned as the result of the U.S. Fifth Circuit Court of Appeals resigned, according to County Superintendent Clyde Muse; all fifteen resignations came from white teachers. In Hinds, under the desegregation plan, 1,485 pupils and 170 teachers were reassigned to new schools. Faculties in the school district were ordered desegregated in order to produce a 55 percent white to 45 percent black ratio in each school to match the ratio in the district as a whole.   In Woodville, no white students appeared at the Woodville Attendance Center on the first day of the court ordered desegregation, "but 471 Negroes did come to enroll at the formerly all-white school in Wilkinson county." According to the January 5, 1970, *Jackson Clarion Ledger*, "White students are reportedly all going or planning to go to a new private school in the process of being organized." In Forrest County, where Hattiesburg is located, a group of nearly "1000 men, women and children marched through a chill drizzle Monday to protest the desegregation plan imposed on Forrest County Public Schools" (*Jackson Clarion Ledger*, January 5, 1970). Jack Robinson, of Citizens for Local Control of Education, told the paper that "what we are fighting is the busing of our children here, there and everywhere over the county to achieve some insane ratio of black and white."   He was referring to the court-ordered desegregation plan in which the ratio of white and black students roughly paralleled that of the population.

In Columbia, the desegregation plan went much smoother. Columbia was one of the 200 schools facing what Governor John Bell Williams called the "moment of decision" in court-ordered classroom desegregation. It went extremely well, "despite 8 youthful pickets whose placards said, 'Hell no, we won't go.'" The principal, told some 600 students to "respect each other, whether in the classroom, on the stairs or in the halls" (*Jackson Clarion Ledger*, January 5, 1970). The school population of blacks increased from 15 to 180. However, desegregation of schools in this city of some 8,000 in southern Mississippi, with about a three to one white to black ratio, was relatively simple compared to rural areas and towns where, according to the paper, "the Negroes outnumber whites and the motto 'never' still applies" (*Jackson Clarion Ledger*, January 7, 1970). In a commentary in the *Jackson Clarion Ledger*, on January 6, 1970, about Canton, where a double system existed in the small central Mississippi town where blacks outnumbered whites three to one, plans led to a new kind of segregated school system by the end of the month; one part was public and primarily for blacks and the second part private and largely white. In Canton, all but "100 of some 1,300 white students in grades one through 12 have registered with the foundation."   The Canton foundation consisted of two schools, one a small facility which has been in existence for five years, and the new school, which is housed in a former tent factory. The foundation recruited teachers "from the public schools, from the ranks of the retired and a few are recent college graduates" (*Jackson Clarion Ledger*, January 6, 1970). Standing against the new white academy was Reverend Luke Mikschi, a white Roman Catholic priest who operated the church black school, who said that "the new foundation is another manifestation of discrimination against blacks" (*Jackson Clarion Ledger*, January 6, 1970). Reverend Mikschi continued, "We give them a year to a year and a half. We've been in the private school business a lot longer than they have and we know. We manage here, but we do it with our sisters, who work for next to nothing" (*Jackson Clarion Ledger*, January 6, 1970).

In Belzoni, State Republican chairman Clarke Reed told a civic group ". . . the social engineers of the Supreme Court and the Fifth Circuit, through their punishment, have subjected us to the worse trial since Reconstruction" (*Jackson Clarion Ledger*, January 6, 1970). He proposed that the immediate goals for the citizenry to remain "calm, seek the most competent persons to serve on school boards and support every means to continue quality instruction" (*Jackson Clarion Ledger*, January 6, 1970). The local leadership was afraid of the racial mixing that was occurring. There was no longer a solution that could be had. One issue that the local whites feared was that not all whites could afford to pay for the private academies. Many of them needed scholarships. The plan to provide scholarships to students failed, as the Fifth Circuit Court ruled it was in violation of the Court's position of desegregation. Mississippi had tried to give tuition waivers to students in the white academies, but such State legislation was repealed. The full effects of desegregation had not been revealed in many school districts because they were still closed for Christmas vacation. Many did not open their doors until January 7, 1970.

On January 7, 1970, as HEW outlined its plan for city pupil mix, whites began the exodus from the public schools. As a Forrest County official told the *Jackson Clarion Ledger*, "we are operating a segregated system now, more than ever. Prior to the court orders, when we were under freedom-of-choice, both races attended schools–now we will teach only Negroes." The county officials reported about 600 of the 4,100 whites in the county schools have either registered or made application for private education. While in Adams County, Natchez school officials said approximately 33 percent of the white students failed to attend orientation activities Monday. In Jackson, a total of 1,485 students were reassigned, effective January 1, and they were to report to their newly assigned schools Tuesday for orientation. Superintendent Clyde Muse of Jackson revealed that the number of reassigned teachers grew to twenty. Like other southern counties, in the Delta County of Adams, sixteen churches voted unanimously to go into the school business. Some 240 students who attended Adams County public schools made applications to attend the new school when it became operational.

In Petal, also in the Delta, the desegregation brought on a sit-in. The paper announced that "fuming white parents and their children staged a sit-in at Petal Junior High Wednesday to protest court orders which moved some 250 white pupils to a previously all Negro school" (*Jackson Clarion Ledger*, January 7, 1970). The paper reported that the ". . . confrontation . . . in an unincorporated community of about 5,000 in Southern Mississippi was the first since 30 school districts started opening Monday under the 'total and immediate' desegregation order of the U.S. Supreme Court" (*Jackson Clarion Ledger*, January 7, 1970). As none of the white students showed up, Principal Loper, described as "a portly gray haired man," gave up "any attempt toward orderly registration of the some 500 pupils, white and Negro, assigned to the school" (*Jackson Clarion Ledger*, January 7, 1970). He said that "about 325 registered Wednesday" (*Jackson Clarion Ledger*, January 7, 1970).

Other counties experienced similar problems. Once again, in Adams County, school officials in Natchez said that "about 58 per cent of the first-day enrollment was Negro" (*Jackson Clarion Ledger*, January 7, 1970). Also, at a meeting held in Columbia Tuesday night, "221 students applied for admission to the proposed West Marion Academy, a private school" (*Jackson Clarion Ledger*, January 7, 1970). Attendance was down in Marion County, where in Columbus, at Marion County High School, a former black school, "opened at 8 a.m. with 45 teachers on hand and 328 11th and 12th grade students reporting for classes. There were 102 whites and 226 Negroes" (*Jackson Clarion Ledger*, January 7, 1970).

In Yazoo City, "twelve fewer Negroes stayed away from the first day of school Wednesday in Yazoo City than did whites"(*Jackson Clarion Ledger*, January 7, 1970). A total of 746, or 367 blacks and 379 whites, "exercised their freedom to stay away from the six public schools here"

(*Jackson Clarion Ledger*, January 7, 1970). Those grades were housed in the formerly predominantly all white Yazoo City Junior High, "with 133 Negroes and 157 whites not attending Wednesday" (*Jackson Clarion Ledger*, January 7, 1970). In Yazoo City, there are "2195 Negroes and 1724 whites" eligible to enroll in public schools, and "on Wednesday 1828 Negroes and 1325 whites enrolled" (*Jackson Clarion Ledger*, January 7, 1970). Yazoo City has a total population of "1071 white children and 2495 Negroes." Many of the white children in school in Yazoo City came from the county. Manchester Academy, which opened in Yazoo City in September, had 500 students through junior high. City leaders had held a series of meetings prior to desegregation and urged public support of the public school system. At Fayette, Mayor Charles Evers charged that whites leaving public schools in Wilkinson, Amite, and Adams Counties were taking books, desks, and other equipment and supplies with them. Evers, the only black mayor of a "biracial municipality in the state," called on both state and U.S. attorneys general to launch an immediate investigation. Evers, who was active in civil rights, said "blacks were unable to support private schools in any form, yet we find down in this area that some merchants have gone on record that they are going to support the private schools." "The only thing," continued Evers, "I can tell my people is that if you really believe in integration and togetherness, don't support those who are going to take your money and use it to divide us" (*Jackson Clarion Ledger*, January 7, 1970).

On January 28, 1970, three days before the February 1, 1970, deadline given by Justice Hugo Black for total desegregation, Senator John Stennis introduced new school legislation, in Washington, that permitted "students and their parents complete freedom of choice in selecting the schools they attend, and also make racial desegregation 'guidelines and criteria' applicable 'uniformly in all regions of the United States'" (*Jackson Clarion Ledger*, January 28, 1970). Once again, Stennis defended Mississippi by attacking what amounted to Freedom of Choice in New York and other northern states. He offered legislation as amendments to the Elementary and Secondary Education Assistance Act (ESEA). It would bar exclusion of a student or students from any public school "on account of race, creed, color or national origin." Stennis told his audience that his "primary purpose is to preserve the neighborhood school." "I emphasize also that this is not an attempt to repeal the Civil Rights Act," declared the

Mississippi Senator. "It is simply a good faith attempt to save the schools of every section of the nation, including the South where they are literally being emasculated in many areas as educational centers for educating their children." Stennis argued that "the education and welfare of the students and teachers have actually become secondary. According to the Senator, "the prime objective has been all-out integration." He emphasized that the South "is actually the sole target of this massive integration program," although there are "segregated conditions in the North that are as pronounced" (*Jackson Clarion Ledger*, January 28, 1970).

Following Stennis' lead, the state of Mississippi decided that the Supreme Court should outlaw the "mix orders." In a January 28 announcement, Governor John Bell Williams charged HEW with violating the Constitution. On January 29, Mississippi filed a U.S. Supreme Court suit to prohibit enforcement of school desegregation orders in the state. On Friday, February 5, 1970, a state delegation met to set a plan to stop desegregation. Five main points were raised, including the dropping of the average daily attendance with a ratio of one black for every two whites. The third problem was that the rearrangement of groups left some students out of the proper grade and age group; e.g., students in grades 1 through 3 with those in grades 9 through 12. The last issue was that in Tunica, no whites showed up to the public schools, and teachers had refused to switch because of their contracts.

On February 7, 1970, a few whites were reporting to "black" schools across the state. According to the Jackson Schools Superintendent, "more than 96% of those who registered last Wednesday showed up for a 'normal first day' in public schools of Jackson Friday." He told the paper that a "total of 34,427 attended classes. That was 88 per cent of the attendance figure on the last full day of school, January 23, when 38,947 were marked present. The registration last Wednesday totaled 35,640" (*Jackson Clarion Ledger*, February 7, 1970). According to a source on the school board, "no incidents were reported. Principals arriving at the administration offices with attendance figures after the regular school day looked pleased and expressed a feeling of pride and accomplishment." However, the Superintendent counted a total of twenty resignations from more than 1,500 teachers.

The school board asked the media to remain outside the schools and not bring attention to desegregation. According to the *Jackson Clarion Ledger*, "local news media honored the school request for no on-campus coverage and waited, for the most part, in administrative headquarters for releases" (February 7, 1970). According to the newspaper, on the seventh of February, a boycott, or at least a semi-boycott, developed in five Jackson secondary schools as the white attendance at the five schools was so slight as to "preclude influenza as the cause, despite its prevalence." The paper stated that "with the exception of those five schools, the full-integration, 'mix-now' plan ordered by the US Supreme Court was declared largely effective." Lanier High, formerly an all-black school, showed the sharpest effect of opposition to the mix. The school listed 294 students as "expected" there; however, only six showed up. Jim Hill High fared a little better; it had 38 whites from an "expected" 177. The figures in the *Jackson Clarion Ledger* show a total of 119 whites appearing out of a total of 957 "expected" to attend classes at the formerly all-black schools (*Jackson Clarion Ledger*, February 8, 1970).

In the state legislature, Senator Bill Alexander estimated "40,000 public school students would not return to public school this semester due to court ordered integration and predicted the figure would be 75,000 next year" (*Jackson Clarion Ledger*, February 8, 1970). Senator Burgen stated that as of January 19, the average daily attendance was down 51,000 from the September average. The paper reported that because of desegregation, private schools were booming. In other words, desegregation remained largely unaccomplished in the thirty Mississippi districts ordered to integrate. In fact, some districts did not comply with the order. Although the rules of the court were being ignored, there was little violence reported around the South. Many parents kept their children home on the February 1 deadline waiting for further developments. In some counties, such as Tallulah, Louisiana, half of the white population enrolled in private academies. In two Mississippi districts, Tunica and Indianola, "some 1,000 white pupils stayed home, with the public schools turning all black." Enrollment at three white private schools in Jackson jumped from 500 to 3,000 between semesters (*Jackson Clarion Ledger*, February 10, 1970).

In order to fight this order, four Dixie governors met during the second weekend of the court order. The conference was announced by John Bell Williams, who had been trying to have a get-together since October of 1969. The conference was held in Mobile, Alabama, and was attended by Lester Maddox of Georgia, Albert Brewer of Alabama, and Louisiana's

John McKeithen. Williams said that "he would be willing to rot in jail if that would do any good. I will fight so long as any individual in the state of Mississippi opposes these acts of judicial dictatorship." Three of the four governors, Brewer, Williams, and Maddox, sought to "tackle desegregation problems through the courts." Brewer and Williams had failed at the Supreme Court level, and Maddox's suit to halt efforts to achieve racial balance in Georgia's schools was still before a federal district court in Washington. According to the paper, "all four have already made it clear that they won't stand for the busing of students to achieve racial desegregation, so it's likely they may have something new to offer following Sunday's session." Only Florida's Claude Kirk, who had "been just as solid in his opposition," had not yet committed to the conference.

Marshall County and Total Desegregation

As a result of total desegregation, schools changed dramatically in the South. Holly Springs was not immune to the change. On February 1, 1970, Holly Springs, where black students outnumbered whites three to one, began the second phase of total desegregation ordered by Justice Hugo Black. "The people here haven't really decided whether they are going to leave the schools or not," stated Holly Springs Superintendent Hollis Morris to the *Jackson Clarion Ledger*. "There is some talk but nothing definite yet. There is a private school here, the Marshall County Education Foundation, and we understand it already has about 350 students attending classes." Holly Springs schools had a first semester enrollment of 573 whites and 1,825 blacks. The schools were registering students on Monday and began classes on Tuesday, February 2, 1970. Morris complained that "the biggest problem we've had has been transferring furniture and equipment and getting classrooms set up. We are making progress and hope to be finished by the weekend." Morris feared that as many as half of the white student body would abandon public schools for private schools. Marshall County Superintendent Stanley Mullikin had similar fears as he stated that "four private schools are in operation in the county, and added that a few white families are known to have moved out of the district." Marshall County had about 1,200 white students and some 3,300 blacks.

Holly Springs experienced similar problems as the rest of the state. School officials believed this change to be temporary. The Holly Springs pullout was believed by some to be temporary, as some 250 of the 500 whites failed to register. The transition was described as moving smoothly, "although eight white teachers resigned, and Negroes were in a 3-1 majority" (*Jackson Clarion Ledger*, February 3, 1970). Holly High did not experience a large dropout in the first year of desegregation, however. That was not the case in the rest of state. In Holly High, many of the parents kept their children in through the first years of total desegregation, choosing to begin to leave only after the end of the first year. By 1973 only 27 white males and 28 white females remained in a class of 97 as compared to 1970. There were 24 black males and 14 females in a class of 99 before desegregation. In 1973, there were only 19 white upperclassmen, including only seven senior females. The Holly Springs case was unique because they only used one white high school, forcing everyone into the same building. In other places it was not so easy, as whites pulled out of the former white schools and refused to attend the former black schools. On Friday, February 5, 1970, the first week's school enrollment figures were released.

Table 9.1 Enrollment in Holly Springs Schools after February 1, 1970,
  Jackson Clarion Ledger

School (grades)	White	Black	Total
Sallie Cochran (1–3)	54	466	520
Frazier/Sims (4–9)	80	960	1040
Holly High (10–12)	69	200	269
Total	203	1680	1880
Difference from First semester	-370	-139	-509
Total First Semester	573	1819	2392
Teachers resigned	8	0	8

Tables 9.1 and 9.2 reveal the large difference in the white enrollment as compared to the black enrollment. In both the city and the county, over half of the white students left the schools. Also, eight teachers left the city

schools. All grades were equally affected by the departures. Because of Marshall Academy's location, in the city, many more elementary school students left the city than the county. The neighboring county of Benton suffered greater white flight than Marshall County, as white students fled the public school system. The February 26, 1970, *South Reporter* reported that all white students assigned to the Ashland School, grades 1 through 2, and 10 through 12, and the Old Salem School, grades 3 through 9, refused to attend on February 23, 1970, in a boycott. Ashland had been about 27 percent integrated before the court case, and Hickory Flat, another school in the county, was not affected because of previous zoning by court order.

Table 9.2 Enrollment in Marshall County Schools after February 1, 1970, the *South Reporter*

School (grades)	White	Black	Total
Galena (1–8)	3	600	603
Slayden (7–9)	24	200	224
Sand Flat (1–6, 10–12)	53	761	814
Byhalia (10–12)	21	211	232
Henry (1–9)	148	1071	1219
Potts Camp (1–3, 8–12)	209	183	392
Mary Reed (4–7)	121	111	232
Total	579	3137	3716
Difference from First semester	-760	-175	-936
Total First Semester	1339	3312	4651

In keeping with the spirit of the desegregation laws of 1970, Principal Joseph Ford decided to keep the two student bodies separate, as if they were still attending two separate schools. Thus, the senior class of 1970, at Holly High, had two student body presidents, one from Sims, and one from Holly High; they also had two yearbooks, and finally, two valedictorians and salutatorians. Co-valedictorians, Eric Hardaway from Sims and Carry Rather from Holly High, gave the address at graduation. The seniors of both schools vowed to finish the year together. That would be the only desegregated school year in Holly Springs. Although in the same school, there was little mingling between the races. The desegregation problem was much easier for the staff, as they accepted the change without overt resistance. Holly High principal Joseph Ford managed adequately, but some things could have been better if they had planned and discussed the changes with the teachers and students. Splendidly, thirty years later, he recalled some of the problems, however.

So when they integrated the school in nineteen seventy, January of seventy . . . there were some things they were doing wrong that probably even made it better for the integration, and what I mean by that is that there was no meeting between teachers, there was no meeting between students before this occurred . . . I blame myself because I was part of the administration . . . you know, I didn't mention this either, but in hindsight it would have been much easier with integration if we had pulled all the teachers together and met with them and then had the teachers talk to students on a first day based upon what our sensibility meeting was about . . . but we didn't do that and yet still integration went kind of smooth, we lost some white children . . .

. . . but if we had done all of the homework we probably wouldn't have lost these children . . . you know, but we didn't do all the homework . . . and myself . . . because I feel like with the teachers that we had . . . if we had kept the children we would have kept some of the teachers, even though Ms. O'Dell stayed until she retired . . . but some of the others did not . . . but see, I think . . . for the type of town, and when I use the word type of town, I mean the background of this town, the old Mr and Mrs. Jane type . . . then I think integration went great because that's a lot of change that had to come about from both sides of the fence . . . particularly the white side . . . because this was something that was new and you know how we don't like to change so fast . . . and this was a change . . . if we had gone in there in the beginning and said we don't want to hear the word nigger, we don't want to hear honkey we don't want to hear white trash, none of this . . . I think we wouldn't have had that . . . but by not doing that we had children fighting each other and we just had to, you know, . . . we had very few problems. . . .

Principal Joseph Ford, who in 1960 was accused of writing inflammatory letters against segregation, was the architect of the desegregation of Holly High. His plan included dividing the three city schools by grade. He recalled that,

I would make the high school nine through twelve and make me principal, and I would put four through eight down at the middle school, five through eight, I told him five, and leave the one through four with Mrs. Belle . . . well they didn't quite do that . . . they did it another way . . . they put ten through twelve and put me up at the high school . . . and they left five through nine . . . a year or so later they added the ninth grade. . . .

The 1970–1971 school year differed significantly from the initial year of desegregation. That fall only about 40 white students returned, leaving 265 white students to 1,781 black students. The high school white population declined from 90 to 56. Ratios of blacks to whites soared. The largest discrepancy appeared at the middle school level, with 991 blacks to 137 whites. The 60 percent of whites that left the schools was the exact number that enrolled at Marshall Academy the next year. The dropout rate for blacks was 70 percent, which increased after desegregation by about 30 percent from the previous 40 percent. Table 9.3 shows the population for the city schools after desegregation. Especially glaring is the low number of white students in the elementary schools. Only city children attended the primary school, as opposed to the intermediate school, which also included children from the outlying areas of the city, especially in the east and south. The low numbers at the elementary level also has to do with the odd separation of 4-4-4, which Principal Ford believed would lead to a better racial balance.

The departure of whites from the schools continued until there were only 32 white males and 28 white females remaining in 1973. That was 20 less than the year before. Whites could leave the public schools and set up a separate school system, and the community could not stop them, as it was a system of private schools. During segregation, whites had an interest in the community schools, although they tended to care more about the white schools. After desegregation, they no longer had any responsibility to the public schools, only to their private schools of choice, yet they still controlled all city and county politics, including the school boards of Marshall County and Holly Springs.

Table 9.3 Holly Springs Public Schools Enrollment, 1970–1971 School
Year, the *South Reporter*

City Schools (grade)	White	Black	Total
Holly High (10–12)	56	307	363
Intermediate (5–9)	137	991	1128
Primary (1–4)	72	483	555
Total	265	1781	2046
Last Year	218	1759	1977
Difference	47	22	69

Along with the rapid change in the student population, Holly High hired nine new black teachers in 1969, adding to the three that had been hired before desegregation as part of the court order to integrate the staffs of the school system. The hiring of these nine teachers is deceiving as the school never replaced the eight teachers it had lost. The first three hired; Charles Gary, Carl Echols, and E.F. Goodman; remained on the staff after desegregation, as well as the two women hired in 1969, Linda Marshall and Hilda Boyd (Interviews, Joseph Ford, June 30, 1999). Joseph Ford, who became principal in 1970 and is today on the county school board, remained at Holly High for twenty years until 1990. By 1972, all class officers were black, and athletics were mostly composed of blacks, as most whites that remained were either the children of schoolteachers or those children whose parents could not afford Marshall Academy or any other private school. During the summer, Holly High changed its team name to Hawks from Tigers, but kept its school colors, green and white. This reflected a racial and school compromise, as Hawks was Sims' choice of name, but maroon and gold were their colors. In December of that year, the school system received excellent news as the elementary school received full accreditation from Southern Association of Colleges and Secondary Schools (SACS), making it one of only 120 schools out of 700 elementary schools accredited in the state of Mississippi.

In order to deal with the 70 percent dropout rate of blacks, Superintendent Frank Ladd received a $114,210 grant in June 1972 to build a vocational education school on the Holly High campus. The total cost for the school would be $450,000. In April 1973, Russell Johnson became principal of the Holly Springs Vocational Education Center. In order to pay for the expenses of the new school building, the Holly Springs School Board asked for 1.5 million dollars in a bond election. The school had old and outdated facilities that were too small, and needed renovation and maintenance, and the high school portables needed to be replaced because they were a fire hazard. The first would be an 18-room addition to the primary school; second the buying of the land next to high school to build a new intermediate school, a new high school with home economics department, covered walkways between the schools, and air conditioning for the primary and intermediate schools and both school cafeterias. The election was held on September 24 for a 13-mill tax. Voters turned down the referendum by a margin of 1,133 to 1,101 (*The South Reporter*, September 25, 1973).

This historic vote signaled the loss of stature of the public schools in the community. Many whites in the community did not recognize the public school system and scorned taxes to support the schools. Holly Springs' whites were tied to their community, attending Holly High generation after generation. Once they left the schools, they abandoned the public school system. Marshall County blacks were in a dire state of poverty and were more worried about employment and food than whether the schools had a new vocational building. The vocational building did open for the 1975 school year. It attracted many night school students, mostly blacks, and became an alternative school for students who did not complete the high school requirements. The stopgap attempt to remedy the high black dropout rate, inadequate funding for facilities, and books left the public school system in disarray. The next section examines some results of the post-civil rights era that shed light on what occurred in Holly Springs because of the rapid change in town.

CHAPTER TEN

Options in the Aftermath of Integration, 1965–1972

Introduction

What were the effects of the desegregation of schools during the Civil Rights Movement in Marshall County? The Movement that began in the 1960s and culminated with the court-ordered desegregation of public schools left two legacies in the area. The first was the involvement of the federal government in the politics and education of the daily life of the people of Marshall County. Marshall Academy, and consequently, the total resegregation of Marshall County and Holly Springs schools, the abandonment of public education by whites for a private system, and the relegation of blacks to an inferior public school system—except one now (in contrast to the old days) controlled by whites who attended the academy and blacks the public schools. This was the legacy of the Civil Rights Movement in the county. Chapter ten examines the influence of the federal government through a history of Head Start, which offered blacks the opportunity to bypass the local political hegemony to receive help in the education of black children. Federal involvement also came with consequences that local blacks did not foresee, such as the loss of local determinism, and the legitimizing of two school systems, one public for blacks and one private for whites. The end of legal segregation had caused blacks to question their role in society, as seen by the conflict in the Head Start program (Marable, 1984; Swift, 1991).

Head Start

The Head Start program in Marshall County exemplifies the struggle between the white leadership of the county and the state to regain the decision-making process from blacks. In the final analysis, the entrenched white ideology and political dominance of its leadership succeeded in taking control away from local blacks. In 1967, Rust College had circumvented the local political and economic white leadership by applying directly to the federal government for $1.5 million from the Office of Economic Opportunity (OEO) through the nation's largest Head Start program, run by Dr. Tom Levin through Child Development Group of

Mississippi (CDGM). The federal grant was paid to the Institute of Community Services (ICS). The Rust College Head Start committee consisted of appointed citizens from Marshall and Lafayette counties. At the time, only a few Head Start centers had been set up in North Mississippi. Marshall County had only three designated Child Development Group of Mississippi (CDGM) centers, one in Holly Springs, one at Byhalia, and one at Potts Camp (Rust College Archives).

CDGM was a grassroots Head Start organization designed to teach lower-economic class students in Mississippi. The organization had achieved independence from both the local schools and the federal government because of the leadership efforts of its director, Tom Levin. He managed to avoid governmental interference by using local resources, such as teachers and community activists. Levin had secured volunteers through an extensive network in the Northeast, by soliciting and receiving support from SNCC and SCLC, by encouraging local leaders, and by employing local blacks as food servers, drivers, and teachers (Dittmer, 1995, pp. 364–382). The program's success also led to its failure. The involvement of civil rights leaders in its ranks attracted conservatives' ire, and led to investigations that resulted in charges of misappropriating funds. The program also paid civil rights workers' fines, and allowed them to use OEO money and property to register blacks to vote (Dittmer, 1995). As John Dittmer (1995) has demonstrated in *Local People*, the Mississippi Democrats, especially John Stennis, used their influence in Congress to broker a deal with President Richard Nixon, who needed his influence over the Foreign Relations Committee to back his foreign policy in Southeast Asia. According to Dittmer, in 1968, Stennis demanded the federal government sacrifice CDGM and Head Start. CDGM was heavily audited, and their money cut. In a matter of one year, CDGM fell apart in North Mississippi.

In 1966, Rust College, in conjunction with the Office of Education and HEW announced two Summer Institutes, first for grades 4 through 6 for six weeks in June and July, and one for grades 7 through 12 from July to August 1966. Under Title XI of the Civil Rights Act, the National Defense Education Act (NDEA) provided money for teachers of disadvantaged youths to attend summer programs that would help them teach better. The federal government held that segregation caused race and class to be intertwined. This connection between the two caused discrimination to occur on two levels, skin color and economic position (Apple, 1979/1990; 1996). As the failure of the mill tax in 1973 to improve the public school facilities demonstrates, after desegregation community support for the schools disappeared. Whites still outvoted blacks and also refused to vote for any tax for the public schools, as they no longer had any interest in it. The newly formed black community had to depend on federal programs such as those sponsored by the NDEA to support the needs of the black community. The Summer Institute and Head Start had several objectives as to the education of blacks in the South. Lacking the economic power and political pressure of the previous year's economic boycott of Holly Springs, the leaders of the Summer Institute believed they offered a great opportunity for the county's teachers. The segregation of the schools made the institute segregated as well. The Institute at Rust was special because for the first time Holly Springs received national attention.

The goal of the Institute was to introduce new techniques for "disadvantaged and disrupted learners" (Rust College Archives, NDEA Summer Institute Proposal, 1966). The new curriculum was developed in the inner city of New York in the late 1960s. The new methodology used the ostensible knowledge of the learner as point of applied instruction (Spring, 1996). The goals of the Summer Institute did not address the economic distress of blacks in the county, overcrowded classrooms, child farm labor, or equal public facilities. The program had three phases: (1) non-grading and effective learning; (2) teaching vocal and quantitative concepts to disadvantaged youths; and (3) problems of teachers in depressed areas (Rust College Archives, NDEA Summer Institute Proposal, 1966). This focus was contradictory to the educational demands made to the city for education in 1965 by the Citizens for Improvement. Those demands centered on issues of equity and access, whereas the Summer Institute demanded separation and exclusion for children because they were different.

Head Start: ICS and Leadership of CDGM

Once again, the formation of a black movement alerted the Sovereignty Commission. On July 25, 1967, Tom Scarbrough contacted authorities in Marshall and Lafayette counties concerning the Institute of Community Services (ICS), the name of the organization that was set up to run Head Start schools in Marshall and Lafayette counties. Eddie Lee Smith, the chairman and former teacher at Rust College, directed the program in the two counties. The Head Start Board of Directors reported that the committee had handled ICS "in a very good manner as compared to the way CDGM has operated" (Sovereignty Commission 2-20-2-60-1-1-1). CDGM had been funded by OEO through Mary Holmes Junior College. According to his sources, Scarbrough reported to the Sovereignty Commission Office that ICS was detouring from the guidelines, which specifically prohibited anyone connected with Head Start programs from participating in political activities either directly or indirectly. This is the same issue that was used to attack CDGM when it paid fines for voter registration instructors, backed black and liberal white candidates, and drove blacks to register to vote.

In July, Scarbrough received a copy of a letter, which established some of the inner workings of the new organization. The letter, "which was copied hurriedly by a person who worked in the Head Start headquarters in Lafayette County," was from a Mrs. Michael Trister to a Mr. Leland Hall. The letter began with a statement of confidence, where she [Mrs. Trister] felt that they would succeed after holding the first organizational meeting, which was attended by every teacher in the program. The goal of the meeting was on what the organization could do for the community. First, they had to follow up on all complaints and make sure they acted on them (Sovereignty Commission 2-20-2-60-1-1-1). The program's leadership believed that this gave "you a little voice in the program, helps to get the administration organized so you don't have to got a different answer from every person on the central staff. Helps in meeting with other groups in the state. Unity speaks in getting group insurance, etc" (Sovereignty Commission 2-20-2-60-1-1-1). The letter also discussed the compensation for teachers. The Head Start Board felt that there was no reason for teachers to have to pay for their meals. That issue was taken to the director and the Head Start Board.

In order to have a voice, the teachers established an employees' executive board made up of one representative from each center that would elect officers, define problems, and call general meetings at all centers and personnel meetings with the administrator. Mrs. Trister, a white outsider from Oxford, was worried that Eddie Smith, a local leader, would not be "very happy about what I am doing" (Sovereignty Commission 2-20-2-60-1-1-1). She complained about the argument that was witnessed by Scarbrough's informant, where Smith told her "about keeping politics out

of education and in turning the people against the administration"
(Sovereignty Commission 2-20-2-60-1-1-1). In the letter, she wrote that
she responded that "Stokely Carmichael only causes trouble when the white
community refuses to listen or denies the outcries from the Negro
community. It will be the same with the center's staff and the
administration. Michael [referring to her husband, an Ole Miss Law
professor] may get a lawyer when the organization is interested in
insurance and investments" (Sovereignty Commission 2-20-2-60-1-1-1).

The Sovereignty Commission's report reveals the infighting that helped
cause the end of the Head Start program as an independent source of
financial aid to blacks. When CDGM was disbanded, local whites charged
that the leadership of Head Start should be under the local schools. One
faction felt it was to educate poor blacks, especially children who were not
getting proper nutrition and care. The other faction, led by outsiders and
the younger members of the local black leadership, felt the organization
should provide leadership in education of blacks, political influence, and
voter registration. This internal division in the political culture of the black
community was invisible to outsiders, but reflected the nationwide trend
that occurred after Stokley Carmichael's 1965 speech in Atlanta about
"Black power." Since Martin Luther King, Jr., had been assassinated in
1968, a power vacuum had existed in the black community, and Carmichael
seemed to move into the role (Paris, 1991). Although there had always
been arguments over where the Movement should go, King had been able
to assert his influence on countless occasions. King had also been the point
of contact for the federal government which gave him a special position for
disseminating information (Katzenbach in Carson,1981/1995, pp. 159-160).

By 1969, the program was dismantled as the old faction of local
leadership was replaced by the new leadership of outsiders, specifically
whites and northern blacks who understood new federal legislation. Eddie
Lee Smith, the director of ICS in Marshall and Lafayette counties, resigned
his position with Head Start on August 1, 1967. Scarbrough believed that
he resigned "because of his dissatisfaction with some of his employees
getting involved in politics" (Sovereignty Commission 2-20-2-60-1-1-1).
Smith also was running for the Marshall County School Board, and
believed that to help the black community, schools had to be integrated
(Interview, Eddie Lee Smith, July 7, 1999). He was succeeded by Arverne
Moore, a former schoolteacher who had been dismissed from his teaching

position. Moore, like Smith, had been active in civil rights activities in Marshall County, participating in marches and boycotts. The new vice-chairman was Quentell Gipson, also a candidate for County Superintendent of Education, and active in civil rights demonstrations and voter registration.

In 1968, after the successful NDEA Institute in the summer of 1966, Rust initiated once again a summer institute for high school teachers. This time the Institute was more aggressive than the one held earlier for elementary school teachers. The NDEA Institute in English for Secondary English Teachers of Culturally-Deprived Youth was acclaimed. The second time around the Institute boasted local black schoolteachers, instead of teachers brought in from the Northeast. This time, however, the Institute only educated thirty teachers because of financial constraints. The objectives had also changed from two years earlier. Instead of focusing on the teaching of self-esteem, the Institute focused on grading, introduced new curricula, taught teachers to use Rockefeller money to enhance their classrooms, and connected the black schools to a local black college or university. The timing of the Institute was also opportune. The South had adopted a testing plan for integration because the Fifth Circuit Court ruled that Freedom of Choice was not causing schools to desegregate. The testing system would take the children with the highest test scores and place them in one school regardless of race. It was not welcomed by whites or blacks, but it was the final stand of Massive Resistance for the schools. The focus of the Institute was on testing and improving test scores of children, in order to match the scores of white students.

The Institute aimed to raise blacks' test scores to show that the U.S. Courts' testing program could work. The county and city schools decided to use testing to integrate schools. Before total desegregation, blacks used the Institute as a tool to help raise black students' test scores, thereby forcing whites to desegregate the schools. According to Smith, that had been the intent of the program from early on, one which he believed was never fully developed. If the system required testing, then the Institute and Head Start should do everything in their power to have black children improve test scores. Smith believed that by improving the test scores of black students, whites would lose another option in keeping schools segregated. Head Start was one aspect of the aftermath of the Civil Rights Movement that was ignored by whites as well as many blacks, not to mention the government. Also ignored was the creation of an all-white private school that offset all the court-ordered rules to integrate.

Marshall Academy

Marshall Academy (MA), supported by the Marshall Academy Education Fund, was founded in 1966 as a private school in the basement of the First Methodist Church of Holly Springs. The support of the Academy came from Senator Yarbrough, the vocal editor of the *South Reporter*. Many members of the community contributed scholarships, financial aid, materials, land, and other essentials to the fledgling school. Marshall Academy was the only school in the county that had a wide support.

The school had an inauspicious start. Lacking money for buildings, it used the First Methodist Church and enrolled no students in the 1967–1968 and 1968–1969 school years. Although Rust was supported by the Methodist church, it did not put up any objections to the use of the First Methodist Church as a school for only whites because no one was attending Marshall Academy. Most whites still seemed to believed that integration would go away. Second, they also trusted testing to assign schools. Whites believed that the blacks could never score higher than whites. Everything changed during the 1969 school year. As the *Anthony vs. Marshall County* case broke in the favor of full desegregation, Marshall was revitalized.

Whites remained in Holly Springs High School for the remainder of the 1969–1970 school year, but then, as the 1970–1971 school year began, only sixty whites remained in grades 9 through 12, including 14 out of 97 seniors in 1973. Apart from the student departures, eight teachers left the schools, five of whom received employment in Marshall Academy. The large influx of students forced Marshall Academy to build a new hundred thousand dollar structure. During the 1970 school year, the school changed from grades 1 through 8 to K through 12 after the winter break. It coincided with the end of legislation and legal actions by the states of Mississippi, Alabama, Florida, Louisiana, and Georgia to stop desegregation. With the influx of students came both cash and clout.

The biggest backer of the private school had been the *South Reporter*, whose editor had several relatives involved with the school, and whose brother, Senator Yarbrough, had fought desegregation. The newspaper slowly began to print more stories about Marshall Academy (MA) sports than about Holly High athletics. For example, as early as October 2, 1969, a homecoming football victory at Marshall Academy received front page headlines, while there was no mention of the Holly Springs High School Homecoming game. In the past, that game and the ceremonies had been one of the highlights of the year along with the Pilgrimage of Homes and the Christmas parade. The paper also announced the first Patriot Day, the name for Homecoming week at the academy. Marshall Academy (MA) tried many different tactics to raise money for the school. One such event was a game between the Jaycees and Lions Club to benefit the Marshall Academy Foundation, which raised money for the school.

In the summer of 1970, Marshall Academy announced plans for two kindergartens because of the overflow of applications for the school. The next day, North Mississippi Academy on Gholson Avenue announced it was beginning classes in September. In an unrelated note in the July 30 *South Reporter*, MA advertised that it was taking donations for scholarships. The academy had its problems. In October 1970, the Internal Revenue Service (IRS) revoked the school's tax exempt status. This move was not all that uncommon for the IRS to punish the white academies in the state. It was the federal government causing a hindrance.

Along the way, Jerry Rubin, who had been the primary civil rights lawyer in the city, was attacked by the newspaper after he criticized the private school. Business was as usual, as the Marshall Academy (MA) Homecoming court made the front page on the same week that Jerry Rubin was being attacked as a troublemaker for mustering blacks to fight against their government. Rubin had taken a case defending blacks who were not allowed to register. These same students at Rust would later file a lawsuit against Circuit Clerk Edward Calicutt. The paper continued this trend of posting Marshall Academy and North Mississippi Academy's announcements and fundraisers, which occurred at one point every week between October 1970 and the summer of 1971. Along with these fundraisers was the popular MA basketball tournament, which made the front page. Marshall Academy (MA) had replaced Holly High as the single most important local institution in Holly Springs for whites. The white community of Holly Springs transferred all loyalty and events from the high school to the academy. The public school was deserted by whites. By 1974, Marshall County and Holly Springs consisted of two groups of people living next to each other who did not live together. The pictures on the hallways of Holly High represented the past, because only children from MA could relate to these photos of their relatives. The kids in the newly segregated desegregated high school had no connection to these pictures except to a past they never knew, since most of them were born fifteen years after the schools were desegregated in 1970.

The Civil Rights Movement in Holly Springs and Marshall County was a long time coming, and took almost twenty years to fully be realized. The Movement began in 1954, and it fizzled out by 1970, after desegregation. Along the way, the city had some unique qualities that separated it from other small towns in the South. It was a central point of focus for the national movement, as Holly Springs was visited by every major organization and dignitary. However, unlike the towns of Greenwood and Selma that gained notoriety for violence, Holly Springs never experienced violence. If there is one word that describes the movement in Holly Springs, it is "politeness." The Civil Rights Movement was a fight for the right to control public space, as blacks tried to gain entree into the propitious mechanism of white society. The main object of their efforts was the public schools. Blacks believed that schools would secure economic and political freedom for their community.

APPENDIX
Desegregation and Holly Springs

Anthony v. Marshall County

In Marshall County, the case that began the issue of desegregation was *Clarence Anthony et al. v. Marshall County Board of Education* (MS No. 26432, U.S. 409 F.2d 1287, 1969), which fell under all precedents set by *Alexander v. Holmes County Board of Education* (396 U.S. 19, 1969). *Clarence Anthony, et al., v. Marshall County Board of Education, et al.* was a class action lawsuit brought back to the court by black school children, represented by their parents on April 15, 1969, in order to desegregate the two public school districts in Marshall County. U.S. District Court for the Northern District of Mississippi, with William C. Keady, Chief Judge, concluded that the "only workable method of bringing meaningful desegregation to schools was to continue under the existing 'freedom of choice' plans." Keady's decision led to the appeal.

At the Court of Appeals, the Circuit Judge held that evidence, including the fact that during the 1967–1968 school term, "only 21 of 1,868 Negro children in one school district and only 22 of 3,606 Negro children in second school district attended white schools, together with the fact that no white students from either district had ever attended a Negro school, established that schools systems remained dual systems and that 'freedom of choice' plans had not been effective in eliminating dual systems, and burden was, therefore, on respective school boards to come forward with realistic and workable plans for effectuating transitions to unitary nondiscriminatory systems." The Court of Appeals reversed and remanded the decision, which left the Board of Education of both Holly Springs and Marshall County filing an appeal to the Fifth Circuit Court.

The precedent used by the Appeals Court Judge Ainsworth was that both *Green v. County School Board of New Kent County, Virginia* (391 U.S. 430, 88, 1968), and *Raney v. Board of Education of Gould School District* (391 U.S. 441, 88, 1968), where the Supreme Court examined "freedom of choice" desegregation school plans adopted by the respondent school boards, and concluded that under the existing circumstances the plans did not constitute adequate compliance with the boards' responsibility under *Brown v. Board of Education of Topeka, Kansas* (349

U.S. 294, 300–301, Brown II, 1955), "to achieve a system of determining admission to the public schools on a nonracial basis." The plan in both aforementioned cases was exactly the same used in Marshall County and Holly Springs. Therefore, it was in violation of the U.S. Supreme Court. In a third case, *Monroe v. Board of Commissioners of City of Jackson, Tennessee* (391 U.S. 450, 88, 1968), a "free transfer" plan was similarly weighed and found wanting under the circumstances of that case. Also, in *United States v. Jefferson County Board of Education* (U.S. 372 F.2d 836, 1966), the Court interpreted this duty as requiring a "unitary school system in which there are no Negro schools and no white schools–just schools."

The Court also followed the recommendations of *Raney v. Board of Education of Gould School District* (391 U.S. 441, 88, 1968), where the Supreme Court threw out a "freedom of choice" plan as unacceptable and required the Board to formulate a new plan, where the evidence showed that "not a single white child had sought to enroll in the all Negro schools, and over 85% of the Negro children in the school system still attend the all Negro schools." In Green, as in the Anthony case, there was no residential segregation, both races residing throughout the county. Also in Green, as in Anthony, despite operation of the respective school systems since 1965 under a "freedom of choice" plan, "not a single white child had expressed a choice to attend a Negro school." In Green, "15% of the Negro students were attending formerly white schools as compared to the much lower figures here of 3.2% in the Holly Springs District and 1.77% in the Marshall County District."

The Anthony case was also held up against *U.S.A. v. Greenwood School District* (U.S. 406 F.2d 1086, 1969), in which the Court, in conformity with Green, held that a "freedom of choice plan" under which less than 6 percent of the black student population attended "has not done the job that is constitutionally required, i.e., the job of converting a dual system into a unitary system in which the separate tracks for Negro and white students are no longer identifiable." The Court held that it was the responsibility of the district courts "to assess the effectiveness of a proposed plan in achieving desegregation."

In the Green case, the U.S. Court stated that, there is no universal answer to complex problems of desegregation; there is obviously no one plan that will do the job in every case. The matter must be assessed in light of the circumstances present and the options available in each instance. It is incumbent upon the school board to establish its proposed plan promises meaningful and immediate progress

toward disestablishing state-imposed segregation. It is incumbent upon the district
court to weigh that claim in light of any alternatives which may be shown as
feasible and more promising in their effectiveness. (391 U.S. 430, 88, 1968)

The second case changing the future of Marshall County and Holly
Springs was *Alexander et al. v. Holmes County Board of Education et al.*
(396 U.S. 19, 1969). The case was assigned on the basis of *Certiorari* to
the United States Fifth Circuit Court of Appeals for the Fifth Circuit, on
October 23, 1969, and decided on October 29, 1969. Judge Hugo Black
stated that the continued operation of racially segregated schools under the
standard of "all deliberate speed" was no longer constitutionally
permissible. "School districts must immediately terminate dual school
systems based on race and operate only unitary schools systems." The
Court of Appeals' order of August 28, 1969, delaying the court's earlier
mandate for desegregation in certain Mississippi school districts was
therefore "vacated and that court is directed to enter an order, effective
immediately, that the schools in those districts be operated on a unitary
basis." According to the Fifth Circuit Court, "while the schools are being
thus operated, the District Court may consider any amendments of the order
which may be proposed, but such amendments may become effective only
with the Court of Appeals' approval." The lower court's decision on the
case was vacated and remanded.

In the Holmes case, Jack Greenberg argued for the petitioners.
Assistant Attorney General Leonard argued for the U.S., and Louis F.
Oberdorfer argued the cause for the Lawyers' Committee for "Civil Rights
Under Law as *amicus curiae* urging reversal." A brief was filed by Richard
B. Sobol and David Rubin for the "National Education Association as
amicus curiae urging reversal." Also, the Tennessee Federation for
Constitutional Government filed a brief as *amicus curiae*. This case
presented an interesting opportunity to settle the school desegregation issue
once and for all. However, it proved fleeting, as there would be more cases
filed as a result of the Court's decision. In a rare *Per curiam* decision, the
Court ruled in favor of Alexander.

This case comes to the Court on a petition for certiorari to the Court of Appeals
for the Fifth Circuit. The petition was granted on October 9, 1969, and the case
set down for early argument. The question presented is one of paramount
importance, involving as it does the denial of fundamental rights to many
thousands of school children, who are presently attending Mississippi schools
under segregated conditions contrary to the applicable decisions of this court.

Against this background the Court of Appeals should have denied all motions for additional time because continued operation of segregated schools under a standard allowing "all deliberate speed" for desegregation is no longer constitutionally permissible. Under explicit holdings of this Court the obligation of every school district is to terminate dual school systems at once and to operate now and hereafter only unitary schools. (Griffin v. School Board, 377 U.S.218, 234 [1964]; Green v. County School Board of New Kent County, 391 U.S. 430, 438–439, 442 [1968]

Accordingly, the court decreed the following:

1. The Court of Appeals' order of August 28, 1969, is vacated, and the case is remanded to that court to issue its decree and order, effective immediately, declaring that each of the school districts here involved may no longer operate a dual school system based on race or color, and directing that they begin immediately to operate as unitary school systems within which no person is to be effectively excluded from any school because of race or color.

2. The Court of Appeals may in its discretion direct the schools here involved to accept all or any part of the August 11, 1969, recommendations of the Department of Health, Education, and Welfare, with any modifications which that court deems proper insofar as those recommendations insure a totally unitary school system for all eligible pupils without regard to race or color.

3. While each of these school systems is being operated as a unitary system under the order of the Court of Appeals, the District Court may hear and consider objections thereto or proposed amendments thereof, provided, however, that the Court of Appeals' order shall be complied within all respects while the District Court considers such objections or amendments, if any are made. No amendment shall become effective before being passed upon by the Court of Appeals.

4. The Court of Appeals shall retain jurisdiction to insure prompt and faithful compliance with its order, and may modify or amend the same as may be deemed necessary or desirable for the operation of a unitary school system.

5. The order of the Court of Appeals dated August 28, 1969, having been vacated and the case remanded for proceedings in conformity with this order, the judgement shall issue forthwith and the Court of Appeals is requested to give priority to the execution of this judgement as far as possible and necessary. (396 U.S. 19, 1969)

Along with the Anthony and Holmes cases, *Carter et al. v. West Feliciana Parish School Board et al.* (396 U.S. 226, 1969), would be the final case that challenged Hugo Black's call for immediate desegregation of the schools. The case went before the Honorable Hugo L. Black, Circuit Justice for the Fifth Circuit, for a temporary injunction order to stop the desegregation of the schools in the Parish. On December 13, 1969, a group of petitioners petitioned for *certiorari* review of a Court of Appeals ruling that authorized a delay in student desegregation in three Louisiana school districts until September 1970. They were granted temporary injunctive relief requiring the "respondent school boards to take the necessary preliminary steps to effectuate complete student desegregation by February 1, 1970," as specified by *Alexander v. Holmes County Board of Education* (396 U.S. 19, 1969). The Court granted the application as the Fifth Circuit Court issued a vacated judgement. In a *Per curiam* decision, Justice Hugo Black, as Circuit Justice for the Fifth Circuit, gave the petitioners a temporary injunctive order and other relief because of three cases that were originally filed in 1965, seeking the desegregation of three Louisiana school districts. Second, according to the orders of the District Courts, in July of 1969, the office of Education of the HEW prepared and submitted terminal desegregation plans for each of the districts here involved for the school year 1969–1970, which were rejected by the District Courts.

Finally, the Singleton case reversed all the United States Court of Appeals for the Fifth Circuit "sitting en banc, on December 1, 1969, subsequent to this Court's decision in Alexander v. Holmes County Board of Education, ante, at 19." The above court ordered respondent school boards and thirteen other school boards to desegregate faculties completely, and to adopt plans for conversion to unitary systems by February 1, 1970, but authorized a delay in pupil desegregation until September 1970. As of February 1, all school districts had to have a plan for total desegregation that had to be implemented by September 1970. This phase served to move the schools into the next phase of desegregation discussed earlier in the Swann case.

Then, on December 10, 1969, petitioners filed in the Fifth Court a petition for a writ of certiorari, together with a motion to advance consideration of the petition and a motion for summary disposition, contending that the decision of the Court of Appeals is inconsistent with this Court's decision in *Alexander v. Holmes County Board of Education* (396 U.S. 19, 1969). The petitioners sought the implementation of the HEW plans for student assignment on or before February 1, 1970, simultaneous with the other steps ordered by the Court of Appeals.

Finally, the application by the petitioners seeking a temporary injunction required that the "respondent school boards, pending a decision by this Court on the merits, to take all necessary clerical and administrative steps– such as determining new student assignments, bus routes and athletic schedules and preparing for any necessary physical changes–preparatory to complete conversion under HEW plans by February 1, 1970. If petitioners were successful, the administrative and clerical tasks necessary to conversion will have been undertaken roughly according to the timetable established by the court below in the Alexander cases, and petitioners' right to effective relief will not have been put in question by the passage of time. If they were unsuccessful in this Court, the school boards would be under no compulsion to convert during this school year." Hugo Black finally granted the petitioners their injunction.

The Judge ordered that, in accordance with *Alexander v. Holmes County Board of Education* (396 U.S. 19, 1969), petitioners' application for a temporary injunctive order requiring the respondent school boards to take such preliminary steps as may be necessary to prepare for complete student desegregation by February 1, 1970. Secondly, by "way of interim relief, and pending this Court's disposition of the petition for certiorari, the judgement of the Court of Appeals is vacated insofar as it deferred desegregation of schools until the school year 1970–1971." Third, by way of interim relief pending further order of the Court, "the respondent school boards are directed to take no steps which are inconsistent with, or which will tend to prejudice or delay, a schedule to implement on or before February 1, 1970, desegregation plans submitted by the Department of Health, Education, and Welfare for student assignment simultaneous with the other steps ordered by the Court of Appeals." The Court also said "respondents are directed to file any response to the petition herein on or before January 2, 1970."

The Court finally placed all cases under *Singleton v. Jackson Municipal Separate School District* (U.S. 419 F.2d 122, 1970). The case involved Derek Jerome Singleton versus the Jackson Municipal Separate School District. The *Clarence Anthony versus Marshall County Board of Education* was also placed under the Singleton case, along with fourteen other cases. The case had been heard in the U.S. Court of Appeals, Fifth Circuit, on December 1, 1969, where judgement was vacated on Dec. 13, 1969. On January 14, 1970, the U.S. Supreme Court reversed the decision, thereby forcing immediate desegregation of schools by February 1, 1970.

The same day, the West Feliciana Parish School Board filed a petition for *certiorari*, which was denied along with the one filed by Jackson Municipal Separate School District.

The Court of Appeals held, *inter alia* (that among other things) since pursuant to United States Supreme Court decision directing that "school districts begin immediately to operate as a unitary school system within which no person is to be effectively excluded from any because of race or color, it would be possible to merge faculties and staff, transportation, services, athletics and other extracurricular activities during present school term," but faced difficulty merging the student body prior to fall term of 1970, would be able to implement a two-step merger plan; the first, including merger of faculties and staff, to be accomplished by February 1, 1970, and the second, including student body merger, to be accomplished by fall term of 1970.

The Court issued fourteen orders, of which the following applied to Marshall County and Holly Springs. "Testing as a basis for assigning students to schools subject to immediate desegregation order cannot be employed until unitary school systems have been established." The Marshall County and Holly Springs suit was seeking to desegregate the two school districts. The district court approved plans that would assign students to schools on the basis of achievement test scores. The Court then decided that it could use testing "in any event until unitary school systems have been established." Thus, all Court cases brought up would be reversed and remanded in favor of the party that can prove that the district is not in compliance with the requirements of *Alexander v. Holmes County* (396 U.S. 19, 1969) and the other provisions and conditions of this order. The Courts would use these cases as a standard to determine how a school system should be desegregated.

The Final Word: The U.S. Supreme Court and Desegregation

Then, on Tuesday, February 8, U.S. District Court Judge James B. McMillan ordered the Charlotte-Mecklenburg school system, the largest in North Carolina, to become desegregated during the spring; elementary schools by April 1, and others by May 4. He ordered the busing of some 10,000 pupils. This case would become the landmark case *Swann v. Charlotte-Mecklenburg,* decided before the Supreme Court in 1971.

Charlotte-Mecklenburg's plan for desegregation was designed by Dr. John Finger, an expert in school administration from Rhode Island College, who was instructed by the U.S. Court to prepare a plan that would reach, to the extent possible and using all available means, a 71:29 ratio of whites to blacks in all schools. He was appointed by the U.S. Supreme Court in December 1969, after the Court rejected the county's desegregation plan as not abiding by the letter of the law. Therefore, in February 1970, the District Court was presented with two plans, the new board plan and the "Finger" plan. The school board closed seven schools and reassigned those students. Second, it redistricted itself to achieve racial balance in the schools, but also rejected popular methods of desegregation, such as pairing and clustering. Instead, they chose to keep the same grade structures. Third, the county merged all athletics into one league, developed a single school busing system, integrated the faculties and staffs of all its schools, and replaced the freedom of choice transfer plan with a minority to majority transfer plan, commonly known as an "m-and-m" transfer.

Today, the m-and-m transfer is the policy where students can attend any school they please out of their assigned feeder pattern school if the racial or ethnic group is underrepresented in that school they choose to attend. The m-and-m transfer is one of the most abused policies in high school athletics, as teams recruit players from around the district and bring them to their school, in order to play basketball. For example, in 1999, the Florida High School Athletic Association leveled a one year ban on Miami Senior High School for illegally recruiting basketball players, a practice that led to six state titles in ten years. Miami High, an 80 percent Hispanic school, recruited two Haitian blacks, two African-Americans, and one white player to play for them, although they were all out of district, using the m-and-m rule. In order for them to come to the school, they were offered gifts and other incentives. The m-and-m rule, intended to equal racial population because of segregation, was used and abused by other parties whose intention was not in the spirit of the law.

The Charlotte-Mecklenberg Board plan proposed the transfer of blacks to nine of the ten high schools in the system, which produced a black population of 20 percent to 40 percent in each school. In the tenth school, the black population would be about 2 percent. At the junior high level, twenty of the twenty-one areas would have a black attendance between one and 40 percent, and in the twenty-first school, in a black area of Charlotte, the population would be about 90 percent. The elementary school problem was immense. Because of the segregation in the neighborhoods, more than half of the elementary schools were over 85 percent black, and about half of the white population was assigned to schools with over 85 percent black.

John Finger's plan was different, in that it required that 300 blacks from the city's black neighborhoods be transported to the all-white Independence High school. He followed the rezoning plan of the board and also created satellite zones whereby inner city blacks were assigned to nine predominately white junior highs, leading to substantial desegregation. The biggest difference lay in the elementary school plan. For the system's seventy-six schools, Finger recommended not using geographic zoning, instead opting for the use of grouping techniques, zoning, and pairing. The result would lead to all elementary schools having between 10 percent and 40 percent blacks in their schools. The city's population was about 70 percent white, and 30 percent black, of which two-thirds lived within the city limits. That was the problem, how to get those students from the city to the suburbs. The District Court adopted the board plan, with the modifications made by Finger for the junior high and high schools. However, the Court rejected the board's plan for the elementary schools, and decided to bus elementary school students around the large Charlotte-Mecklenberg system. The Court of Appeals agreed with the plan for the junior and senior high, but "vacated" the order relating to the elementary schools. The Court decided that the buses used to transport the children have direct routes. The students would be picked up at schools near their homes, and then directly transported to their school. The Supreme Court discovered that the average trip was seven miles, and would take over thirty-five minutes. The Court summarized its brief with the statement that "Desegregation plans cannot be limited to the walk-in school." Therefore, busing, as an extension of the school's public facilities, can be used to achieve desegregation.

In Georgia, similar situations to those in Charlotte occurred. For example, in Washington County, schools planned to open Monday under a new plan of faculty desegregation after 48 of the 68 white teachers boycotting the system during the week decided to return to work. In Bibb County, schools remained unchanged because Judge Alexander Lawrence had not ruled on the integration plans submitted to him. However, the paper predicted that this was the tip of the iceberg, as "even greater numbers of Southern school districts are facing September desegregation deadlines as a result of other court orders."

REFERENCES

Primary Sources

U.S. Department of Education Documents, 1954–1976

U.S. Federal Government Documents on Civil Rights, 1946–1980

U.S. Supreme Court Records, 1960–1972

U.S. Census, 1950

U.S. Census, 1960

U.S. Census, 1970

U.S. Census, 1980

U.S. Census, 1990

Civil Rights Act of 1964

Voting Rights Act of 1965

State of Mississippi Archives, Jackson, Mississippi

State of Mississippi Statistical Abstracts, 1960–1980

State of Mississippi Sovereignty Commission Records, 1956–1977

State of Mississippi Blue Book, 1960–1980

State of Mississippi Report on Education, 1960–1980

State of Mississippi Attorney General Biennium Report, 1963–1969

SACS Reports, Marshall County School System, 1956–1970

SACS Reports, Holly Springs Separate School System, 1956–1970

University of Mississippi Archives

Rust College Archives

Holly High Springs High School Yearbooks, 1964–1974

Holly High Springs High School Attendance Reports, 1967–1970

Marshall County Archives

Holly Springs Archives

Jackson Clarion Ledger

The South Reporter

Court Cases

Anthony et al. v. Marshall County Board of Education et al. (Mississippi No. 56432, U.S. 409 F.2d 1282, 1969).

Alexander v. Holmes County Board of Education (396 U.S. 19, 1969).

Bowman v. County School Board of Charles City County (U.S. 382 F.2d 326, 333, 1967).

Brown v. Board of Education of Topeka, Kansas (349 U.S. 294, 300–301, Brown II, 1955).

Carter et al. v. West Feliciana Parish School Board et al. (396 U.S. 226, 1969).

Green v. County School Board of New Kent County (U.S. 430, 88 S.Ct. 1689, 20 L.Ed.2d 716, 1968).

Green v. County School Board of New Kent County, Virginia (391 U.S. 430, 88, 1968).

Monroe v. Board of Commissioners of City of Jackson, Tennessee (391 U.S. 450 88, 1968).

Raney v. Board of Education of Gould School District (391 U.S. 441, 88, 1968).

San Antonio Independent School District v. Rodriguez (411 U.S. 1, 93 S. Ct. 127, 1973).

Singleton v. Jackson Municipal Separate School District (U.S. 419 F.2d 122, 1970).

Swann v. Charlotte-Mecklenberg (402 U.S. 1, 1971).

T.H. Stubbs et al. vs. Marshall County Citizens for Progress (MS Chancery Court, No. 10,869).

U.S.A. v. Greenwood School District (U.S. 406 F.2d 1086, 1969).

United States v. Jefferson County Board of Education (U.S. 372 F.2d 836, 1966).

Interviews

Donnal Ash	Bobby Mitchell
Al Beck	Faunta O'Dell
David Caldwell	Leon Roundtree
Joseph Ford	Tommy Smith
Charles Gary	Eddie Lee Smith
Ruth Harper Greer	Lorrie Swanee
Greg Gresham	Sandra Young
Jesse Jackson	

Secondary Sources

Anderson, B. (1991). *Imagined Communities*. London: Verso.

Anderson, V. (1995).   *Beyond Ontological Blackness*.   New York:
Continuum.

Apple, M. (1979/1990). *Ideology and Curriculum.* New York: Routledge.

Apple, M. (1996). *Cultural Politics and Education.* New York: Teachers
College Press.

Arendt, H. (1968). *Men in Dark Times*. New York: Brace, Harcourt and
World.

Arendt, H. (1970). *On Violence*. New York: Brace, Harcourt and World.

Arendt, H. (1994). *Eichmann in Jerusalem*. New York: Penguin.

Arendt, H. (1995). *On Revolution*. New York Penguin.

Arendt, H. (1998). *The Human Condition*. Chicago: University of Chicago
Press.

Argyris, C., & D. Schon. (1974).   *Theory in Practice*.   San Francisco:
Jossey-Bass.

Baker, L.D. (1998).   *From Savage to Negro: Anthropology and the
Construction of Race, 1896–1954*. Berkeley: University of California
Press.

Baker, R.S. (1973). *Following the Color Line: An Account of Negro
Citizenship in the American Democracy*. Williamstown, MA: Corner
House Publishers.

Baldwin, J. (1955). *Notes of a Native Son*. Boston: Beacon Press.

Baldwin, J. (1961). *Nobody Knows My Name: More Notes of a Native Son.* New York: The Dial Press.

Bandura, A. (1977). *Social Learning Theory.* Englewood Cliffs, NJ: Prentice Hall.

Bartley, N. (1969). *The Rise of Massive Resistance: Race and Politics in the South During the 1950s.* Baton Rouge: Louisiana State University Press.

Bartley, N. (1995). *The New South, 1945–1980.* Baton Rouge: Louisiana State University Press.

Beabout, G. (1996). *Freedom and Its Misuses: Kierkegaard on Anxiety and Despair.* Milwaukee: Marquette University Press.

Bellah, R. (1985). *Habits of the Heart: Individualism and Collectivism in American Life.* Berkeley: University of California Press.

Bennis, W., et al. (1961). *The Planning of Change.* New York: Holt/Rinehart.

Bernard, H.R. (1995). *Research Methods in Anthropology.* London: Altamira Press.

Bertelson, D. (1967). *The Lazy South.* New York: Oxford University Press.

Black, E. (1976). *Southern Governors and Civil Rights: Racial Segregation as a Campaign Issue in the Second Reconstruction.* Cambridge: Harvard University Press.

Blackbourn, D., & G. Eley. (1984). *Mythen Deutscher Geschichtsschreibung.* New York: Oxford University Press.

Blotner, J. (1974). *Faulkner: A Biography.* Vol. 1, New York: Random House.

Bordieu, P. (1990). *In Other Words*. Palo Alto, CA: Stanford University Press.

Bullock, H.A. (1970). *A History of Negro Education in the South*. New York: Praeger.

Burton, O. (1985). *In My Father's House Are Many Mansions: Family and Community in Edgerfield, SC*. Chapel Hill, NC: University of North Carolina Press.

Camus, A. (1991). *The Rebel: An Essay on Man in Revolt*. A. Bower (Trans.). New York: Vintage International.

Carson, C. (1981/1995). *In Struggle: SNCC and the Black Awakening of the 1960s*. Cambridge, MA: Harvard University Press.

Carspecken, P.F. (1996). *Critical Ethnography in Educational Research: A Theoretical and Practical Guide*. New York: Routledge.

Childress, J. (1971). *Civil Disobedience and Political Obligation*. New Haven: Yale University Press.

Cobb, J. (1982). *The Selling of the South: The Southern Crusade for Industrial Development, 1936–1980*. Baton Rouge: Louisiana State University Press.

Cobb, J. (1984). *Industrialization and Southern Society, 1877–1984*. Lexington, KY: University Press of Kentucky.

Cobb, J. (1992). *The Most Southern Place on Earth: The Mississippi Delta and the Roots of Regional Identity*. New York: Oxford University Press.

Cohen, W. (1991). *At Freedom's Edge: Black Mobility and the Southern White Quest for Racial Control, 1861–1915*. Baton Rouge: Louisiana State University Press.

Cohodas, N. (1997). *The Band Played Dixie: Race and the Liberal Conscience of Ole Miss.* New York: The Free Press.

Colapietro, V. (1989). *Peirce's Approach to the Self.* Albany, NY: State University of New York Press.

Cooper, W.J., Jr., & T.E. Terrill. (1991). *The American South: A History.* New York: Alfred Knopf.

Coser, L.A. (1952). Social Conflict and the Theory of Social Change. *The British Journal of Sociology*, 7, 197–205.

Critchley, S. (1997). *Very Little . . . Almost Nothing: Reason, Philosophy and Literature.* New York: Routledge.

Curry, C. (1995). *Silver Rights.* Chapel Hill, NC: Algonquin Books.

Daniel, P. (1985). *Breaking the Land: The Transformation of Cotton, Tobacco and Rice Cultures since 1880.* Urbana, IL: University of Illinois Press.

Degler, C. (1977). *Place over Time: The Continuity of Southern Distinctiveness.* Baton Rouge: Louisiana State University.

Dewey, J. (1963). *Freedom and Culture.* New York: Capricorn Books.

Dillard, G. (1994). *Private Battles, Culture Wars: White Southern Writers and the Movement for Black Civil Rights.* Doctoral Dissertation, Florida State University.

Dittmer, J. (1995). *Local People: The Struggle for Civil Rights in Mississippi.* Urbana, IL: University of Illinois Press.

Dohrenwend, B.S., & S.A. Richardson. (1965). Directiveness and Nondirectiveness in Research Interviewing: A Reformulation of the Problem. *Psychology Bulletin*, 63, 475–485.

Du Bois, W.E.B. (1995). *The Souls of Black Folk.* New York: Signet.

Eagles, C. (Ed.). (1986). *The Civil Rights Movement in America.* Jackson, MS: University of Mississippi Press.

Eaton, C. (1969). *The Mind of the Old South.* Baton Rouge: Louisiana State University Press.

Ellison, R. (1994). *Invisible Man.* New York: Modern Library.

Emmanuel, S. (1996). *Kierkegaard and the Concept of Revelation.* Albany, NY: State University of New York Press.

Fanon, F. (1967). *Black Skin, White Masks.* New York: Grove Press.

Faulkner, W. (1929/1992). *The Sound and the Fury.* New York: The Modern Library.

Faulkner, W. (1964). *Absalom, Absalom!* New York: The Modern Library.

Fick, C.E. (1993). *The Making of Haiti: The Saint Domingue Revolution from Below.* Knoxville, TN: University of Tennessee Press.

Fields, B. (1985). *Slavery and Freedom on the Middle Ground: Maryland During the Nineteenth Century.* New Haven: Yale University Press.

Fischer, D.H. (1971). *Historians' Fallacies: Toward a Logic of Historical Thought.* London: Routledge.

Fite, G. (1984). *Cotton Fields No More: Southern Agriculture, 1865– 1980.* Lexington, KY: University Press of Kentucky.

Fleming, J., & Gill, G., & Swinton, D. (1978). *The Case for Affirmative Action for Blacks in Higher Education.* Washington, DC: Howard University Press.

Ford, M., & S. Kincaid. (1963). *Who's Who in Faulkner.* Baton Rouge: Louisiana State University Press.

Foster, G. (1987). *Ghosts of the Confederacy: Defeat, the Lost Cause, and the Emergence of the New South, 1865 to 1913.* New York: Oxford University Press.

Foucault, M. (1970). *The Order of Things.* New York: Pantheon.

Foucault, M. (1977). *Discipline and Punish: The Birth of the Prison.* A. Sheridan (Trans.). New York: Pantheon.

Foucault, M. (1980). *Power/Knowledge.* New York: Pantheon.

Franklin, J.H. (1968). *The Militant South, 1861–1865.* Cambridge, MA: Harvard University Press.

Fredrickson, G. (1995). *Black Liberation.* New York: Oxford University Press.

Freire, P. (1970). *Pedagogy of the Oppressed.* New York: Continuum.

Freire, P. (1994). *Pedagogy of Hope.* New York: Continuum.

Fromm, E. (1941). *Escape from Freedom.* New York: Holt.

Gaston. P.M. (1970). *The New South Creed: A Study in Southern Mythmaking.* Baton Rouge: Louisiana State University Press.

Gavins, R. (1977). *The Perils and Prospects of Southern Black Leadership: Gordon Blaine Hancock, 1884–1970.* Durham, NC: Duke University Press.

Genovese, E. (1974). *Roll, Jordan, Roll: The World the Slaves Made.* New York: Pantheon Books.

Goldfield, D.R. (1990). *Black, White, and Southern: Race Relations and Southern Culture, 1940 to the Present.* Baton Rouge: Louisiana State University.

Gollnick, D., & P. Chinn. (1994). *Multicultural Education in a Pluralistic Society.* Upper Saddle River, NJ: Merrill.

Goodwyn, L. (1976). *Democratic Promise: The Populist Movement in America.* New York: Oxford University Press.

Gorden, R.L. (1975). *Interviewing: Strategy, Techniques, and Tactics.* Homewood, IL: Dorsey.

Gramsci, A. (1997). *Selections from the Prison Notebooks of Antonio Gramsci.* Q. Hoare and G. Smith (Eds. & Trans.). New York: International Publishers.

Greenfeld, L. (1992). *Nationalism: Five Roads to Modernity.* Cambridge: Harvard University Press.

Gutman, H. (1976). *The Black Family in Slavery and Freedom, 1750–1925.* New York: Pantheon Books.

Habermas, J. (1971). *Knowledge and Human Interests.* Boston: Beacon.

Habermas, J. (1973). *Theory and Practice.* J. Viertel (Trans.). Boston: Beacon.

Hacker, A. (1992). *Two Nations: Black and White, Separate, Hostile, Unequal.* New York: Scribners.

Hall, J.D. (1987). *Like a Family: The Making of a Southern Cotton Mill World.* Chapel Hill, NC: University of North Carolina Press.

Harvey, P. (1997). *Redeeming the South.* Chapel Hill, NC: University of North Carolina Press.

Hendrickson, R. (1990). *The Civil Rights Movement in American Fiction: A Feminist Reading.* Doctoral Dissertation, Brandeis University.

Hicks, J. (1931). *The Populist Revolt: History of the Farmers' Alliance and the People's Party.* Minneapolis, MN: University of Minnesota Press.

Hoffer, E. (1951/1989). *The True Believer.* New York: Harper & Row.

Hoffer, E. (1963). *The Ordeal of Change.* New York: Harper.

Hurston, Z.N. (1995). *The Complete Stories.* New York: Harper Collins.

I'll Take My Stand. (1928). New York: Harper & Row.

Jacoway, E., and Colburn, D. (Eds.). (1982). *Southern Businessmen and Desegregation: Civil Rights and the Changing South.* Baton Rouge: Louisiana State University Press.

Janiewski, D. (1985). *Sisterhood Denied: Race, Gender, and Class in a New South Community.* Philadelphia: Temple University Press.

Jaspers, K. (1954). *Way to Wisdom: An Introduction to Philosophy.* R. Manheim (Trans.). New Haven: Yale University Press.

Jaspers, K. (1961). *The Future of Mankind.* E.B. Ashton (Trans.). Chicago: University of Chicago Press.

Jenkins, L. (1981). *Faulkner and Black-White Relations: A Psychoanalytic Approach.* New York: Columbia University Press.

Jordan, W. (1968). *White over Black: American Attitudes Toward the Negro, 1550–1812.* New York: Norton.

Jordan, W. (1974). *The White Man's Burden: Historical Origins of Racism in the United States.* New York: Oxford University Press.

Key, V.O., Jr. (1949). *Southern Politics in State and Nation*. New York: Alfred Knopf.

Killens, J. O. (1965). *Black Man's Burden*. New York: Pocket Books.

Kirby, J.T. (1987). *Rural Worlds Lost: The American South, 1920–1960*. Baton Rouge: Louisiana State University Press.

Kozol, J. (1967). *Death at an Early Age; the Destruction of the Hearts and Minds of Negro Children in the Boston Public Schools*. Boston: Houghton Mifflin.

Kreyling, M. (1998). *Inventing Southern Literature*. Jackson, MS: University of Mississippi Press.

Lee, G. (Ed.). (1967). *Crusade Against Ignorance: Thomas Jefferson on Education*. New York: Teachers College Press.

Lenin, V. (1970). *On Culture and Cultural Revolution*. Moscow: Progress Publishers.

Lewin, K. (1948). *Resolving Social Conflicts*. New York: Harper & Row.

Loewen, J.W. (1971). *The Mississippi Chinese; Between Black and White*. Cambridge: Harvard University Press.

Mandle, J. (1978). *The Roots of Black Poverty: The Southern Plantation Economy after the Civil War*. Durham, NC: Duke University Press.

Marable, M. (1983). *How Capitalism Underdeveloped Black America: Problems in Race, Political Economy, and Society*. Boston: South End Press.

Marable, M. (1984). *How Capitalism Underdeveloped Black America: Problems in Race, Political Economy, and Society*. Second Edition. Boston: South End Press.

Marable, M. (1989). *Race, Reform, and Rebellion: The Second Reconstruction in Black America.* Jackson, MS: University of Mississippi Press.

Marable, M. (1999). *Black Leadership.* New York: Penguin Books.

Marshall, F.R. (1967). *Labor in the South.* Cambridge: Harvard University Press.

Martin, B.L. (1991). From Negro to Black to African American: The Power of Names and Naming. *Political Science Quarterly*, 106(1), 83–107.

Martin, T. (1976). *Race First: The Ideological and Organizational Struggles of Marcus Garvey and Universal Negro Improvement Association.* Westport, CT: Greenwood Press.

Maslow, A. (1968). *Toward a Psychology of Being.* Princeton, NJ: Van Nostrand.

McKinney, J.C. (1965). *The South in Continuity and Change.* Durham, NC: Duke University Press.

McMillen, N. (1989). *Dark Journey.* Chicago: University of Illinois Press.

Morgan, E. (1998). Writing Black History, in *New York Review*, 14–26.

Morris, A.D. (1984). *The Origins of the Civil Rights Movement: Black Communities Organizing for Change.* New York: Free Press.

Morris, W. (1971). *Yazoo: Integration in a Deep-Southern Town.* New York: Harper's Magazine Press.

Morrison, J. (1967). *W.J. Cash: Southern Prophet.* New York: Alfred Knopf.

Morton, P. (1991). *Disfigured Images: The Historical Assault on Afro-American Women.* Westport, CT: Greenwood Press.

Myrdal, G. (1944). *An American Dilemma: The Negro Problem and Modern Democracy.* New York: Harper and Brothers.

Namorato, M. (1979). *Have We Overcome? Race Relations since Brown.* Jackson, MS: University of Mississippi Press.

Namorato, M. (1998). *The Catholic Church in Mississippi, 1911–1984: A History.* Westport, CT: Greenwood Press.

Nielson, M. (1989). *Even Mississippi.* Tuscaloosa, AL: University of Alabama Press.

Nieto, S. (1997). *Affirming Diversity.* New York: Longman.

Novick, P. (1988). *That Noble Dream: The "Objectivity Question" and the American Historical Profession.* Cambridge, England: Cambridge University Press.

O'Brien, M. (1979). *The Idea of the American South, 1920–1941.* Baltimore, MD: Johns Hopkins University Press.

Osofsky, G. (1967). *The Burden of Race.* New York: Harper.

Osterweis, R. (1971). *Romanticism and Nationalism in the Old South.* Baton Rouge: Louisiana State University Press.

Osterweis, R. (1973). *The Myth of the Lost Cause, 1865–1900.* Hamden, CT: Archon Books.

Paris, P. (1991). *Black Religious Leaders: Conflict in Unity.* Louisville, KY: John Knox Press.

Parks, E.W. (1970). *Southern Poets.* New York: Pantheon.

Polk, N. (1997). *Outside the Southern Myth*. Jackson, MS: University of Mississippi Press.

Popper, K. (1984/1992). *In Search of a Better World*. New York: Routledge.

Potter, D.M. (1968). *The South and the Sectional Conflict*. Baton Rouge: Louisiana State University Press.

Potter, D.M. (1972). *The South and the Concurrent Majority*. Baton Rouge: Louisiana State University Press.

Potter, D.M., & T.G. Manning. (Eds.). (1949). *Nationalism and Sectionalism in America, 1775–1877: Select Problems in Historical Interpretation*. New York: Holt.

Reed, J.S. (1972). *The Enduring South: Subcultural Persistence in Mass Society*. Lexington, MA: Lexington Books.

Reed, M.L. Hough, & G. Fink. (1981). *Southern Workers and Their Unions, 1880–1975*. Westport, CT: Greenwood Press.

Reed, M.E. (1991). *Seedtime for the Modern Civil Rights Movement: The President's Commission on Fair Employment Practice, 1941–1946*. Baton Rouge: Louisiana State University Press.

Rosengarten, T. (1974). *All God's Dangers, the Life of Nate Shaw*. New York: Knopf.

Schrag, O.O. (1971). *Existence, Existenz, and Transcendence*. Pittsburgh: Duquesne University Press.

Silbermann, C. (1968). *Crisis in Black and White*. New York: Random House.

Silver, J. (1966). *Mississippi: The Closed Society*. New York: Harcourt/Brace.

Sitkoff, H. (1981). *The Struggle for Black Equality.* New York: Hill and Wang.

Smith, C., & Miller, M. (1998). *Marshall County.* Dover, NH: Arcadia Publishing.

Sowell, T. (1981). *Ethnic America.* New York: Basic Books.

Spradley, J.P. (1979). *The Ethnographic Interview.* New York: Holt.

Spring, J. (1996). *American Education.* Seventh Edition. New York: McGraw-Hill.

Stuckey, S. (1987). *Slave Culture: Nationalist Theory and the Foundations of a Black America.* New York: Oxford University Press.

Swift, J. (Ed.). (1991). *Dream and Reality: The Modern Black Struggle for Freedom and Equality.* New York: Greenwood Press.

Taulbert, C.L. (1989). *Once upon a Time We Were Colored.* Tulsa, OK: Council Oak Books.

Thomas, E. (1971). *The Confederacy as a Revolutionary Experience.* Englewood Cliffs, NJ: Prentice-Hall.

Thompson, E.P. (1963). *The Making of the English Working Class.* New York: Vintage Books.

Tindall, G.B. (1964). Mythology: A New Frontier in Southern History. In F. Vandiver (Ed.), *The Idea of the South: Pursuit of a Central Theme.* Chicago: University of Chicago Press, 1–16.

Tindall, G. (1975). *The Persistent Tradition in New South Politics.* Baton Rouge: Louisiana State University Press.

Tindall, G. (1976). *The Ethnic Southerners.* Baton Rouge: Louisiana State University Press.

Triandis, H. (1995). *Individualism and Collectivism.* Boulder, CO: Westview Press.

Walker, A. (1982). *The Color Purple.* New York: Pocket Books.

Warren, R.P. (1961). *The Legacy of the Civil War.* New York: Random House.

Weber, M. (1961). *Basic Concepts in Sociology.* Translated by H.P. Secher. New York: Citadel Press.

Weiner, J. (1978). *Social Origins of the New South: Alabama, 1860–1865.* Baton Rouge: Louisiana State University Press.

Weisbord, R. (1973). *Ebony Kinships: Africa, Africans, and the Afro-American.* Westport, CT: Greenwood Press.

Wharton, V. (1947). *The Negro in Mississippi, 1865–1890.* Chapel Hill, NC: University of North Carolina Press.

Whitman, M. (1998). *The Irony of Desegregation Law.* Princeton, NJ: M. Wiener.

Wieder, A. (1997). *Race and Education.* New York: Peter Lang.

Williamson, J. (1993). *William Faulkner and Southern History.* London: Oxford University Press.

Wolters, R. (1970). *Negroes and the Great Depression.* Westport, CT: Greenwood.

Wolters, R. (1984). *The Burden of Brown: Thirty Years of School Desegregation.* Knoxville, TN: University of Tennessee Press.

Woodward, C.V. (1951). *Origins of the New South.* Baton Rouge: Louisiana State University Press.

Woodward, C.V. (1974). *The Strange Career of Jim Crow*. New York: Oxford University Press.

Woodward, C.V. (1993). *The Burden of Southern History*. Baton Rouge: University of Louisiana Press.

Wright, R. (1993). *The Outsider*. New York: Harper.

Wright, R. (1998). *Black Boy*. New York: Perennial Classic.

Wyatt-Brown, B. (1984). *Southern Honor: Ethics and Behavior in the Old South*. New York: Oxford University Press.

INDEX

A

Aberdeen, Mississippi, 80
Africa, 11,12
African-Americans, 5, 7, 113, 135
Africanness, 14
Alabama, 14, 46, 58, 96, 111, 125
Alexander v. Holmes County Board of Education, 128, 130, 132, 133, 134
Alexander, Bill, 111
Altman, Robert, 5
Amite, Mississippi, 109
Anderson, Benedict, 5, 9
Anderson, William H., 64, 65, 72
Anthony, Clarence, 76
Anthony, et al. v. Marshall County Board of Education, et al., 29, 73, 82, 125, 128, 129, 131, 133
Appalachian Mountains, 14
Appleton, H. B., 34, 35, 36, 37, 41, 52
Arendt, Hannah, 5,8, 10, 11, 15
Argyris, Chris, 16
Asbury Methodist Church, 10, 43, 50, 51
Ash, J.M. "Flick," 36, 44, 51 52, 57, 58, 69
Ashland School, 59, 114
Atlanta, Georgia, 1, 96, 123
Atlantic City, New Jersey, 52

B

Baker, Lee D. 2
Beck, Al, 74, 87, 88, 89, 90, 93, 96, 97, 99
Bell, Alice, 86, 116
Bell, Osborne, 1
Bellah, Robert, 4, 6
Benne, Kenneth, 15, 17
Bennis, Warren, 15
Bennett, J. D., 67
Benton County, Mississippi, 36, 38, 49, 50, 67
Berry, Elwood, 53

Black community, 7, 9, 10, 15, 19, 40, 47, 55, 61, 62, 63, 89, 90, 121, 123
black identity, 6, 7, 9, 10, 13, 15, 18
Birmingham, Alabama, 1, 4, 21, 88
Black, Hugo, 73, 83, 109, 112, 130, 131, 132 133
Black Power, 7, 123
Black Zionism, 11, 14
Blaylock, W. V., 44
boll weevil, 21
Boston, Massachusetts, 4
Bourdieu, Pierre, 16
Bowman v. County School Board of Charles City County, 77
Boycott 3, 33, 34, 35, 36, 39, 45, 47, 49, 50, 53, 55, 56, 57, 60, 61, 62, 63, 64, 65, 66, 67, 68, 70, 72, 75, 111, 114, 121, 124
Boyd, Henry, 41, 50, 56, 72, 75
Boyd, Hilda, 117
Brewer, Albert, 111
Brittenum Funeral Home, 22
Brittenum, J.F., 38
Brown v. Board of Education of Topeka, Kansas, 3, 6, 8, 44, 59, 102, 128, 129
Brown II, 40, 75, 77, 102, 129
Brooks, Nat, 75
Bryant, Harold, 34
Buchanan, Jim, 34, 38, 39
Bullock, Henry Allan, 14
busing, school, 66, 79, 112, 134, 136
Byhalia, Mississippi, 22, 52, 66, 72, 84, 86, 114, 120

C

CADET (Christian Aided Development through Extraordinary Training Individualized for Each), also known as St. Mary or St. Joseph, 29, 31, 39, 63, 76, 90

Freedom School, 10, 41, 48, 49, 50, 75
Freedom Summer (of 1964), 49, 54
Freire, Paulo 16

G

Galena, Mississippi, 86, 114
Garvey, Marcus, 11, 14
Gary, Charles, 117
Georgia, 21, 1121, 11,, 125, 136
Gettysburg, Pennsylvania, 12
Gipson, Quentell, 70, 124
Goodman, E.F., 117
Gramsci, Antonio, 5, 9, 16
Grant, Ulysses S., 21, 100
*Green v. County School Board of New
    Kent County*, 38, 77, 128, 131
Greensboro, North Carolina, 38
Greenwood, Mississippi, 52, 96, 127
Greer, Ruth, 52, 74, 87, 88, 91, 92, 93,
    94, 95, 98
Grenada, Mississippi, 21, 40, 74

H

Hall, Leland, 122
Hardaway, Eric, 115
Harvey, Paul, 9
Hattiesburg, Mississippi, 40, 47, 104, 106
Hawkins, Ben, 57
Head Start, 4, 31, 68, 1119, 120, 121,
    122, 123, 124
Henry High School, 40, 84, 86, 114
HEW (Department of Health, Education,
    and Welfare), 62, 79, 84, 85, 103,
    105, 107, 110, 120, 132, 133
Hickory Flat, Mississippi, 114
Hill-Burton Hospital, 41
Hillcrest Cemetery, 22
Hinds, Mississippi, 105
Holly High Tiger Yearbook, 74
Holly Springs, Mississippi, 1, 2, 3, 4, 5, 6,
    7, 10, 18, 19, 20, 21, 22, 23, 24, 26,
    29, 34, 35, 36, 37, 38, 39, 40, 41, 42,
    43, 44, 45, 46, 47, 48, 49, 50, 51, 52,
    53, 54, 55, 56, 57, 58, 59, 60, 61, 62,
    63, 64, 65, 67, 70, 71, 72, 74, 75, 76,
    78, 79, 80, 81, 82, 83, 84, 85, 86, 87,

Holly Springs, Mississippi (continued)
    88, 93, 94, 95, 97, 99, 100, 102, 112,
    113, 115, 116, 117, 118, 119, 120,
    125, 156, 127, 128, 129, 130, 134
    Board of Aldermen, 61
    Board of Education, 61
    Board of Trustees, 81
    Elementary School, 74, 76, 77, 80,
        81, 82, 84, 85, 86, 113
    Garden Club, 2, 35, 45
    High School (Holly High), 23, 35,
        36, 45, 74, 75, 78, 82, 84, 85, 86, 87,
        88, 89, 91, 93, 96, 97, 113, 114, 115,
        117, 118, 125, 126, 127
    Intermediate School, 86, 116, 118
    Vocational Education Center, 118
Houston, Texas, 1
Hurston, Zora Neale, 13

I

ICS (Institute of Community Service)
    120, 121, 122, 123
Imagined Communities, 5, 9, 12
Indianola, Mississippi, 111

J

Jackson, Mississippi, 47, 52, 71, 104,
    108, 110, 111
    Municipal Separate School District,
        83, 111, 133, 134
Jackson Clarion Ledger, 3, 104, 106, 107,
    110, 111, 112, 113
Jackson, Lester, 1
Jacoway, Elizabeth, 100
Jaycees, 126
Jim Crow, 13, 64
Johnson, Lyndon, 13
Johnson, Russell, 118
Jones, Albert, 34, 36, 38, 41, 44
Jones and McElwain Foundry, 21
Jones, Hermit, 104
Jim Hill High, 111

K

Keady, William, 76, 77, 79, 80, 82, 84,
    128

N

NAACP (National Association for the Advancement of Colored People), 1, 17, 33, 36, 37, 38, 43, 44, 48, 63, 64, 68

Nation of Islam, 75

NDEA (National Defense Education Act), 120, 121

    Institute, 124

    Summer Institute, 124

Nero, S.T., 38, 43

New Kent County, 38

New South, 1

New York, 58, 79, 88, 109, 121

Natchez, Mississippi, 83, 104, 107, 108

Newsom, W. W., 71

North Carolina, University of, 15

North Mississippi, 2, 20, 21, 22, 34, 48, 67, 120

North Mississippi Hospital, 42

O

Office of Economic Opportunity (OEO), 119, 120, 122

Old Salem School, 114

Old South, 1

Oxford, Mississippi, 1, 22, 70, 71, 122

P

Pairing, School, 82, 83, 135, 136

Park Avenue, 23

Parker Schoolhouse, 52

Pasadena, California, 105

Pasadena School District Mix Suit, 105

PTA (Parent Teacher Association), 63

Payne, William Sidney, 69

Peirce, Charles, 11

Petal, Mississippi, 108

Polk, Charley, 69

poll tax, 41, 42, 102

Pontotoc, 1836 Treaty of, 20

Potts Camp, Mississippi, 22, 63, 84, 86, 114, 120

R

Randolph, Donald, 86

Raney v. Board of Education of Gould School District, 128, 129

Rankin, Ed, 43

Rather, Carry, 115

Red Banks, Mississippi, 49

Reeves, Henry, 38

Regional Council of Negro Leadership, 38

resegregation, 72, 119

Reynolds, Modina, 74

Riggin, C. L., 42

Ripley, Mississippi, 57

Robinson, Jack, 106

Robinson, Skip, 58, 61, 63, 64, 65, 66, 68, 72, 75

Rosenwald School, 40

Rotary Club, 35

Roundtree, Leon, 71, 72

Roxie, Mississippi, 13, 94

Rubin, Larry, 51, 52, 53, 126

Rust Avenue, 22, 57, 58, 88

Rust College (Rust), 2, 3, 5, 10, 22, 23, 25, 26, 29, 31, 32, 35, 37, 43, 44, 45, 48, 49, 53, 55, 56, 57, 58, 59, 60, 61, 64, 65, 71, 72, 74, 75, 100, 119, 120, 121, 122, 125, 126

S

SACS (Southern Association of Colleges and Secondary Schools), 117

St. Joseph (see CADET)

St. Mary (see CADET)

Sallie Cochran Elementary (see Holly Springs Elementary School)

Sand Flat School, 40, 84, 86, 114

Scarbrough, Tom, 34, 35, 36, 37, 38, 39, 40, 41, 42, 43, 44, 45, 46, 47, 48, 49, 51, 52, 53, 55, 56, 57, 58, 65, 67, 68, 69, 121, 122, 123

Schon, Donald, 16

SCLC (Southern Christian Leadership Council), 7, 44, 120

Second Reconstruction, 15

Selma, Alabama, 4, 58, 74, 76, 127

Senatobia, Mississippi, 22